MW01148787

THE COMMUNICATION
EFFECT

THE COMMUNICATION EFFECT

How to Enhance Learning by Building Ideas and Bridging Information Gaps

Jeff Zwiers

FOR INFORMATION:

Corwin

A SAGE Company

2455 Teller Road

Thousand Oaks, California 91320

(800) 233-9936

www.corwin.com

SAGE Publications Ltd.

1 Oliver's Yard

55 City Road

London EC1Y 1SP

United Kingdom

SAGE Publications India Pvt. Ltd.

B 1/I 1 Mohan Cooperative Industrial Area

Mathura Road, New Delhi 110 044

India

SAGE Publications Asia-Pacific Pte. Ltd.

18 Cross Street #10-10/11/12

China Square Central

Singapore 048423

Program Director and Publisher:
  Dan Alpert

Content Development Editor:
  Lucas Schleicher

Senior Editorial Assistant: Mia Rodriguez

Project Editor: Amy Schroller

Copy Editor: Megan Markanich

Typesetter: Hurix Digital

Proofreader: Dennis W. Webb

Indexer: Nancy Fulton

Cover Designer: Scott Van Atta

Marketing Manager: Maura Sullivan

Copyright © 2020 by Corwin

All rights reserved. Except as permitted by U.S. copyright law, no part of this work may be reproduced or distributed in any form or by any means, or stored in a database or retrieval system, without permission in writing from the publisher.

When forms and sample documents appearing in this work are intended for reproduction, they will be marked as such. Reproduction of their use is authorized for educational use by educators, local school sites, and/or noncommercial or nonprofit entities that have purchased the book.

All third party trademarks referenced or depicted herein are included solely for the purpose of illustration and are the property of their respective owners. Reference to these trademarks in no way indicates any relationship with, or endorsement by, the trademark owner.

Printed in the United States of America

Library of Congress Cataloging-in-Publication Data

Names: Zwiers, Jeff, author.

Title: The communication effect : how to enhance learning by building ideas and bridging information gaps / Jeff Zwiers.

Description: Thousand Oaks, California : Corwin, 2020. | Includes bibliographical references and index.

Identifiers: LCCN 2019025925 | ISBN 9781544375557 (paperback) | ISBN 9781544394060 (epub) | ISBN 9781544394114 (epub) | ISBN 9781544394152 (adobe pdf)

Subjects: LCSH: Communication in education. | Interaction analysis in education. | Classroom environment. | Teacher-student relationships.

Classification: LCC LB1033.5 .Z949 2020 | DDC 371.102/2—dc23

LC record available at https://lccn.loc.gov/2019025925

This book is printed on acid-free paper.

19 20 21 22 23 10 9 8 7 6 5 4 3 2 1

DISCLAIMER: This book may direct you to access third-party content via Web links, QR codes, or other scannable technologies, which are provided for your reference by the author(s). Corwin makes no guarantee that such third-party content will be available for your use and encourages you to review the terms and conditions of such third-party content. Corwin takes no responsibility and assumes no liability for your use of any third-party content, nor does Corwin approve, sponsor, endorse, verify, or certify such third-party content.

Contents

Visit the companion website at
https://resources.corwin.com/Communication Effect
for downloadable tools and resources.

Acknowledgments

I would like the thank the many educators with whom I have collaborated and learned from over the years: Candice Bennett, Theresa Blanchard, Timothy Boals, Magda Chia, Leslee Cybulski, Vinci Daro, Gil Diaz, Jack Dieckmann, Anastasia Difino, Gabriel Enriquez, Sue Fotopoulos, Maria Friedland, Dania Ghrawi, Claude Goldenberg, Margo Gottlieb, Kenji Hakuta, Sara Hamerla, Bonnie Hansen, Tara House, Linda Hoyt, Patrick Hurley, Kentaro Iwasaki, Adria Klein, Nicole Knight, Nancy Ku, Annie Camey Kuo, Robert Linquanti, Cindi Lyon, Preetha Krishnan Menon, Catherine O'Connor, David Pearson, Gina Ramirez, Octavio Rodriguez, Tonya Ward Singer, Kristin Stout, Gabriela Uro, and Steven Weiss.

Special thanks go to my family for their love, devotion, and patience during the writing of this book.

Dr. Jeff Zwiers is a senior researcher at the Stanford University Graduate School of Education. He supports the Understanding Language initiative, a research and professional development project focused on fortifying literacy, cognition, discourse, and academic language. His current research focuses on effective lesson planning and classroom practices that foster lasting learning.

Of all the life skills available to us, communication is perhaps the most empowering.

—Bret Morrison

Language was invented to express meaningful ideas, solve important problems, and get things done. It tends to serve these purposes quite well in every arena of life except the one where it matters the most: school. Somehow, in the effort to standardize, list, and optimize learning, typical lessons have been stripped of the highly engaging purposes that language needs in order to thrive. The authentic communication that is so essential to our development as humans has been squeezed out to make room for a highly processed, fast-food version of learning that is limiting our students' capacities to grow and thrive.

Content learning (e.g., math, science, history) also suffers when instruction lacks authentic communication and is instead driven by long lists of facts, concepts, and skills to memorize for tests. In my research and work in schools, I have noticed that content teaching is more effective when students communicate to get things done with language rather than communicate just to get points and grades. Students' writing, retention of knowledge, and engagement (based on student interviews) as well as teacher reflections (based on interviews) showed significant results (in content and language learning) when students were communicating to build up meaningful ideas in the discipline. But in the average lesson on a typical day, robust idea building is more the exception than the rule. A lot of content instruction is still designed to help students memorize a myriad of loosely connected facts, skills, topics, and standards for getting lots of right answers on easy-to-score tests.

Language development was never meant to be separated from content learning, nor vice versa. Yet too many English language arts (ELA) and English language development (ELD) curriculums have sliced and diced language into long and disconnected lists of grammar rules and linguistic labels. These pieces have then been "organized" into workbook exercises, quizzes, and tests. And most language programs have sacrificed the use of interesting, deep, and consistent content over time in order to cover and assess the linguistic pieces. I have observed too many language lessons in which the students were asked to memorize how the language works instead of actually using it to construct meaning. Such a behaviorist view of learning doesn't value students as thinkers and learners.

I have spent the past decade collaborating with a wide range of teachers on improving student learning in their classrooms. During this time, I have observed hundreds of lessons and learned from countless conversations with teachers about what was working and not working in their lessons to foster deep and lasting learning of content and language. I interviewed dozens of students on what kinds of tasks in school fueled their desire to learn without being rewarded with points or grades. On the weekends, I pored over hundreds of resources, books, articles, and research studies, and in my spare time I analyzed lesson plans, approaches, practices, activities, and analyses of student work that researchers, teachers, and students found to be effective. The most salient common element that emerged from this decade of work was a set of three features that, when combined, make up what I call *authentic communication*.

This book, therefore, describes enhancements that teachers can do in every lesson to make the principal modes of communication (reading, listening, speaking, writing, conversing) more authentic. These changes will result in a more powerful learning in your setting—guaranteed or your money back.

FOUNDATIONAL THINKERS

Famous educators, past and present, have called for similar changes in how we do school. Unfortunately, their calls have not been answered well enough. Their ideas have had a profound influence on the ideas in this book. If I were to cite them all in the following chapters in every spot where they have had some influence, the book would be much longer. So I include their foundational ideas here in highly condensed versions. As you read through this book, you will see how their ideas are put into practice. One hope that I have for this book is that it will honor these educators and their efforts to improve education over the years.

John Dewey and Experience-Based Learning

Over a century ago, Dewey was pushing back against memorization and disconnected learning, instead proposing what he called a directed living and experience-based approach. This view focused on having students participate in real-world-esque "workshops" in which students could collaborate, voice their ideas, and think for themselves. Dewey valued student agency for learning and as a result of learning. He wrote, "Education, therefore, is a process of living and not a preparation for future living" and "Give the pupils something to do, not something to learn; and the doing is of such a nature as to demand thinking; learning naturally results" (Dewey, 1916, p. 191). (See also Dewey, 1938.)

Lev Vygotsky and Co-Constructing Knowledge

Vygotsky wrote, "By giving our students practice in talking with others, we give them frames for thinking on their own" (Vygotsky, 1978, p. 19). He argued that learning is a social and cultural process in which children co-construct knowledge with others. They learn by actively doing rather than by passively observing. As students work with others, they bring unique and often "rough drafts" of knowledge and skills that they hone as they engage in meaningful tasks with others. To Vygotsky, communication was essential for development.

He emphasized that using language with others influences the inner language that people use to think. He wrote, "Every function in the child's cultural development appears twice: first, on the social level and, later on, on the individual level; first, between people (interpsychological) and then inside the child (intrapsychological). This applies equally to voluntary attention, to logical memory, and to the formation of concepts. All the higher functions originate as actual relationships between individuals" (Vygotsky, 1978, p. 57).

Vygotsky's (1978) ideas also got us thinking about appropriately challenging students in what is called a student's zone of proximal development (ZPD). A student's ZPD is the set of skills and concepts to be learned that are just beyond what he or she can do independently. One of the essential purposes of authentic communication is getting students to push themselves and others to use language as effectively as possible, to operate within the ZPD as much and as often as possible because they are building something with language. (See also Vygotsky, 1986.)

Jerome Bruner and the Role of Social Interaction

Influenced by the ideas of Vygotsky, Bruner also argued that social interaction plays a key role in a child's development of language and cognition. For Bruner, learning needed to be active and social. Bruner is also known for being one of the originators of the term *scaffolding*. He wrote, "The world is indeed full of facts. But facts are not of much use when offered by the hatful—either by teacher to student in class, or in the reverse direction as name dropping in an 'objective'" (Bruner, 1996, p. 55). He also wrote, "Truths are the product of evidence, argument, and construction rather than of authority, textual or pedagogic" (p. 57). (See also Wood, Bruner, & Ross, 1976.)

Courtney Cazden and Student-Initiated Discourse

One of the field's most respected experts on classroom discourse, Cazden argued back in 1977, "Language is learned, not because we want to talk or read or write about language, but because we want to talk and read and write about the world . . . especially for children, language is the medium of our interpersonal relationships, the medium of our mental life, the medium of learning about the world" (p. 42). She also emphasized moving past the common discourse model, IRE, which entails teacher *initiation* of talk, student *response* to it (often short answers), and *evaluation* by the teacher. The teacher often does much more of the talking in this format, and students' building of ideas is limited. (See also Cazden, 2001.)

What all of these educators have in common is an unwavering passion for students—especially those students who have been marginalized by "traditional" teaching and assessment practices. They emphasize the important role that language plays in learning as well as the key role that socioemotional factors play in overall development. And they highlight the importance of authenticity in learning. Much of what you will read in this book is based on the core ideas and principles that they emphasized in order to foster deeper and more lasting learning of content, language, thinking, and life skills.

THE COMMUNICATION EFFECT

As you have likely gathered by now, the communication effect is the combination of all the differences that happen as a result of enhancing instructional activities with key features of authentic communication. These differences include deeper learning of content concepts and skills, richer understandings of the perspectives of others, improved language skills, increased student ownership of learning, and more engagement. In addition to these student differences, you will also notice the positive effect that improved student communication has on teacher morale and development. Most of us became teachers in order to use our creativity, expertise, and passion to help students blossom into the unique and brilliant people they were meant to be. It feels good to be serving our students in authentic, enduring, respectful, and human ways.

The challenge that this book is trying to address is significant: enhancing instruction in all lessons in ways that maximize the learning effects of high-quality communication in the classroom. It's a lot of work, as you will see, but not attempting to address this challenge will tend to allow current trends of inequity, lack of engagement, shallow content learning, and below-grade-level literacy to continue. I work with many teachers who say that it's worth the work. They have come to see that inauthentic communication, or "pseudo-communication," as I call it, was limiting the potential learning of students—and this was especially true for students who use language in ways that differ from the ways that schools expect.

We are all wired for using language to create, build, and share ideas. Most entering kindergartners, at just five years of age, speak their home language fluently, in complete sentences, using a wide range of words and sentences. And yet, these children cannot tell you a single grammar rule, have never studied a list of words for a quiz, and haven't been forced to use sentence stems posted on the walls in their bedrooms. So how do little kids get so fluent without expensive language textbooks and fill-in-the-blank drills, or even being able to read? They use language to communicate. They use it to meet their needs and express their thoughts.

At this point please make a mental note that, even though most of the examples in this book are in English, the ideas and suggestions apply to teaching and learning in all languages and forms of communication. The goal is to improve students' abilities to communicate as strongly and clearly as possible, which could mean that they use a wide and creative range of languages, tools, and skills in order to get the job done.

Communicating to Learn and Communicating to Others

Authentic communication serves two major overlapping roles in school. One role is to foster learning, which means that students authentically read, write, listen, speak, and converse in order to build up enduring ideas of value in a discipline. Helping students to do this is the main focus of Chapters 3 through 7 in this book. Another major role, when the idea is built up enough, is communicating it to others. This type of communicating often takes the form of a project, paper, article, presentation, poster, web page, or some other performance task that allows students to logically put together the key blocks of an idea into something that is useful to others. Communicating to others tends to help the others learn, and it helps the person communicating to learn as well (usually even more than the others). There are many examples of enhancing the communication of ideas to others in the following chapters.

INTENDED AUDIENCE

This book was written mainly for teachers, but instructional coaches, administrators, and curriculum designers will benefit from it too. Most of the classroom examples come from four content areas: ELA, math, science, and history, in Grades 3 through 9, where I have spent the bulk of my time coaching teachers and coteaching with them. This book's ideas are also useful for teachers of ELD or English as a second language (ESL) and other language classes because language, paradoxically, thrives the most when it is not the focus. It thrives when students strive to use it to do things, create, argue, and even play with it in order to discover what meaningful ideas can emerge.

The ultimate beneficiaries of this book are students. Even though all students will likely benefit from the ideas and enhancements in these pages, I wrote this book with the following students in mind:

- Students who often just "play the game" of school

- Students who don't want to play the game of school

- Students who face extra academic challenges because they are still developing proficiency in using English for academic purposes

- Students with diverse cultural backgrounds and learning paradigms that differ from what and how school expects them to learn and show learning

- Students with diverse and special needs who can benefit from more and better communication at school

- Students who need more practice putting their academic ideas into words and are reticent to push themselves to use language

- Students who aren't motivated enough by points and grades

- Students in schools and classrooms that struggle to engage students in learning

BOOK OVERVIEW

Chapter 1 provides an in-depth discussion of authentic and pseudo-communication, outlining the three features of authentic communication that guide all of the suggested recommendations throughout later chapters. Chapter 2 presents ideas for how to cultivate a classroom culture where authentic communication can thrive. Chapters 3 through 7 detail how specific instructional activities that emphasize reading, listening, speaking, writing, and conversing can be enhanced in order to offer rich and robust opportunities for authentic communication. These chapters also include detailed classroom examples to show how teachers used the enhancements in a lesson. Chapters 5 and 6 include Going Deeper sections that describe related, novel teaching activities that have been enhanced enough to use tomorrow. Finally, Chapter 8 caps off the book with a look at how we all can leverage four dimensions of teacher creativity to meet the challenges of addressing the authenticity challenge.

Here is a quick overview chart of the enhanced activities in Chapters 3 through 7.

Chapter 3 Reading	Chapter 4 Listening	Chapter 5 Speaking	Chapter 6 Writing	Chapter 7 Conversing
• Teaching of comprehension strategies • Close reading • Text feature walks and talks • Reading of word problems	• Think-pair-shares • Read-alouds • Listening to presentations • Listening to math instruction	• Think-pair-shares • Jigsaws • Gallery walks • Shared problem solving in math	• Writing workshops • Shared and collaborative writing • Use of writing organizers • Peer editing, review, and feedback	• Whole-class discussions • Small-group conversations • Paired conversations • Socratic seminars

As you can see, these are commonly used activities across grade levels and content areas. With a focus on communication, some might ask why this book doesn't just focus on language classes (ELA, ELD, ESL, etc.). Authentic communication is powerful in these classes, but other content areas, as I and others often argue, tend to have (a) even more need for it and (b) lots of untapped potential for developing language used for building up and expressing academic ideas. This is because the brain likes to build and it likes to connect. History, science, and math classes are full of fascinating and important ideas to build up through authentic communication.

Throughout the past ten years, I have had a wide range of meaningful conversations with teachers. Many of the questions that emerged in these conversations became the initial seeds of this book. Some of these guiding questions are as follows:

- How can we facilitate enduring learning of content, language, and thinking?
- What are the most effective ways to foster my students' socioemotional growth?
- How can I effectively teach students with a wide range of language proficiencies at the same time?
- How can we get students to do more than the bare minimum and engage more often and more deeply in learning activities?
- How can we provide students with more agency, voice, and choice in what and how they are learning?
- How can we best prepare students for higher education and life?
- How can we modify existing curriculums and assessments to meet the needs of our students?

The answers to these questions are not more long checklists of instructional strategies, or telling students they just need to persevere and believe they can learn, or having higher expectations, or expensive computer programs, or new grading systems, or the latest district initiative to raise test scores. The answers to these questions are rooted in improving authentic communication in the classroom. We are at a fork in the road, a time in which we can, with some extra effort and creativity, significantly improve instruction for decades to come.

A MAJOR OVERHAUL

The changes to instruction, assessment, and curriculum that are described in the following chapters are large and time consuming. Oh, and there are many ideas in the following pages that clash with common practices in most schools around the United States and the world. These common practices tend to promote learning that is neat, clean, linear, and easily visible and countable. Yet the learning promoted in this book can't easily be checked off on a list, and it can't easily be tested with multiple-choice tests. It tends to be messy and impossible to organize with pacing guides. It is visible, but it takes a lot of work and time to see. Yet at the end of each unit and each year, the deep and enduring learning is worth it, as I am hoping you and your students will see.

I am also hoping that by the end of this book you will see how the choices and enhancements described in this book can make big differences in the lives of students. And I am hoping that you will try some of the enhancements out in your setting in order to directly see these differences in your students. I also hope that this book helps you to make authentic communication a foundational cornerstone in your evolving pedagogy.

Perhaps my biggest hope is that you will see the urgency of this major "overhaul." A great many students who need the most communication experiences are placed in classes where they get them the least. Test-focused teaching methods and tracking (which is often informed by testing) have deprived millions of students of high-quality opportunities to communicate extensively with other students who are extremely rich and engaging sources of language and knowledge. In the zeal to level and track certain students, too many of them are cut off from engaging and robust curriculums from which they could benefit immensely.

It's time to start amplifying and deepening students' learning by setting up classrooms in which students want to push themselves to communicate authentically. When this happens, students will be much better equipped and inspired to grow into the amazing people they were meant to become.

FROM PSEUDO- TO AUTHENTIC COMMUNICATION

The student mind yearns to be a growing, bustling city of ideas.

If you could hear the thoughts of students in a typical lesson in a typical class-room, what would you hear? Some students might be thinking, "This is inter-esting. I need to learn this. I'm looking very forward to the eventual test on what I am learning." Yet other students might be thinking other thoughts, such as "What do we have to do today? How little can I do to get the points I need? Will this be on the test? Will it be graded? What's for lunch? She's coming over here. I need to look like I'm working. I'll never use this. This is boring." Unpro-ductive and disengaged thoughts such as these are natural and, in small doses, are not a problem.

The problem emerges when thoughts like these become the norm during les-sons across grade levels, content areas, and the years. They add up quickly and can seriously hinder learning, especially for students in schools that do not effectively meet their learning needs. Yes, large numbers of students will keep doing well in school regardless of instructional quality. But students who are less academically successful, many of whom use language in ways that don't neatly line up with the expectations of school tasks, dont and won't do as well in typical "learn this or else you won't get your points" lessons.

I am not talking about success on tests, which is often mistakenly called achievement. I am talking about true achievement, which is a mixture of social and emotional development, academic knowledge and skills development, creativity and language development. This mixture, which varies across students, helps them build good relationships, perform well in the workplace, have more choices in life, and make better choices. Based on my analyses of the research, classroom observations, and work with teachers, I am convinced that true achievement for students with whom we tend to be most concerned stems in large part from engaging in authentic communication in school.

A HUGE CHALLENGE: PSEUDO-COMMUNICATION IS THE NORM

Pseudo-communication is the use of language for purposes *other than* doing something meaningful. These purposes are usually focused on getting something: points; grades; attention; praise; or, oftentimes, simply to avoid upsetting the teacher. Yet when students are focused on rewards rather than on building up something meaningful, they tend to do just enough to get what they want. Many students have figured out how to talk, write, read, listen, and converse as little as possible, staying off the radar, year after year after year. They know how to play the "game of school," paying for points with answers and assignments, usually just going through the motions of communication.

Here are several student comments that exemplify this problem:

- An eighth grader, walking out of his history class, said, "It's like we're robots. They tell us what to learn and then we gotta show it on those boring tests. And then I forget it all the next day."

- A fifth grader looks at a writing rubric and asks, "What do I have to do now to get 3s or 4s on each row?"

- Two third graders, after reading the same story, are asked by the teacher to engage in a pair-share that summarizes what happened. Neither student tries to listen or speak very much. I ask why they don't say more and one student says, "I know what she knows, like, for the summary. So why talk?"

While these examples seem minor, they add up. Consider how differently these students will learn if, instead, year after year they have the following thoughts. For the eighth-grade history student, we should want him to think, "My teachers are asking me to think like a historian and to build up important ideas about history that will serve me for years to come." For the fifth-grade writer, we should want her to think, "How can I best communicate my idea in writing to my reader(s)? This rubric has some good suggestions for helping me communicate my idea as clearly and strongly as possible." And for the students engaged in pair-shares, we should want them to think, "Pair-shares are great opportunities to share our unique opinions, information, and evidence in order to co-construct important ideas and engage in work beyond this interaction." Yes, I know their thoughts won't likely sound exactly like these, but it gives us a rough goal to work toward.

For decades, pseudo-communication practices have wormed their way into the fabric of daily teaching and assessment in our schools. Most of these practices even *seem* to be authentic on the surface because they have been done in classrooms for so long. Writing essays, taking tests, answering chapter questions, solving problems, filling in worksheets, creating group posters, reading aloud, giving oral presentations, sharing in pair-shares, etc.,…this *is* school, right? Yet if you take a closer look, these are often meant less to truly communicate and more to show students' learning as well as keep them busy and controlled. Students know this, so it isn't a surprise that they focus on pleasing the teacher more than truly communicating to build up and express ideas.

The longer you do something a certain way, the harder it is to change. Whether or not typical school practices today directly descended from "factory models" of a century ago, it doesn't matter. Many lessons and assessments do have a factorylike framework in which large numbers of students are "filled" with the same facts and skills as efficiently and cheaply as possible. Students then take "as cheaply as we can score them" tests to allegedly show this learning or not. With such a long history of this type of learning—and with only slight variations of it (often called pockets of excellence) here and there—educators and students have gotten used to pseudo-communication, thinking that this is what school is. Students think, "I show up. I read things and answer questions, I write essays with a checklist, and I get my points. This must be learning."

One problem with pseudo-communication-heavy lessons is that they can and do produce some learning, or at least the appearance of it, especially when looking at multiple-choice tests. When test scores go up a little, many teachers, administrators, and students don't see a need to make any major changes. They will consider the effort it takes to overhaul how we teach and learn to be unnecessary or too risky. Some tend to think, "What we're doing works well enough. Why rock the boat?" And yet, what we are doing in many settings is not working well enough for too many of our students.

Lost Potential and Missed Opportunities

Another problem emerges when we think about teaching practices over time. One week or unit, or even year, is not hugely formative or damaging when it comes to the effects of pseudo-communication in the classroom. But over multiple years, and especially over the thirteen-year stretch of K–12 schooling, it can make a big difference whether the bulk of the communication in lessons was authentic or not. When students have a do-the-bare-minimum, go-through-the-motions approach to learning each day of school, learning tends to just hobble along. If they haven't pushed themselves or pushed their peers to clarify or support their ideas—for example, to say more than one word or sentence when sharing their ideas—then they can miss out on thousands of opportunities to practice putting their thoughts into words. These missed opportunities add up.

Consider a typical fifth grader, Alondra. Alondra walks into a classroom, sits at her desk, and gets her language arts book out. She turns to page 37, which shows a picture of a turtle on a beach, and the teacher starts modeling a reading strategy called making inferences. She is instructed to practice this strategy as she reads and then must answer three inference-based questions about the text. The teacher asks, "What inferences did you make?" Alondra doesn't want to answer, but her name stick is drawn, and she quickly comes up with something to say. She says something that sounds enough like an inference for the teacher to move on.

Or take a typical ninth grader, David. He walks into his algebra class, watches the teacher solve a couple of problems about lines and equations, and then works with a partner to solve six more problems from the book. He doesn't see the usefulness of it all, but this is school. He doesn't love math, and he doesn't hate it. It is just another hour of school to him.

There are many students like Alondra and David, and there are many lessons like the ones described. This point-based approach to learning, even though it is so common, tends to severely limit the potentials of student growth.

Now imagine doubling, tripling, or even quadrupling the amount of time that all students spend thinking about major concepts in each discipline. And imagine Alondra and David highly engaged in communicating what they are thinking and learning. Think of the potential for expanding their thinking and language abilities when they push themselves to learn rather than be pushed to demonstrate their learning. And think about the rich learning that all students might experience when teachers and assessments value their unique ways of building and communicating robust ideas.

Learned Helplessness

A related problem that I have noticed in spending lots of time in classrooms is a variation of "learned helplessness" in the field of psychology (Seligman, 1972). The term originated from experiments on animals that stopped trying some action or activity when they learned that it didn't make a difference at all with respect to the rewards being given. Students can exhibit this, too, when they start to think, "Whether I take the energy to communicate (or be communicated to) or not, or whether I do more than the bare minimum or not, the rewards aren't that different. I may get a slightly higher grade for working to communicate, but it's not worth the effort, so the bare minimum it is." Even if just one student thinks on a regular basis, it's a big problem.

Many approaches, strategies, and curriculum guides continue to rely on activities that lack authentic communication. In this book, I argue that we need to (a) notice pseudo-communication in its many forms, (b) be bothered by it, and (c) make some significant changes as a result. This means, at whatever pace we can manage, we should be designing and enhancing our practices to have more potential for authentic communication. We do this so that, whatever comes our way in the future—new standards, new curriculum guides, new students, new leadership, new tests, or new technology—a powerful pedagogical cornerstone (not just a tool) will be helping students learn through and for authentic communication.

AUTHENTIC COMMUNICATION

Authentic communication, in a nutshell, means interacting with one or more other people to do something meaningful with language. By language I mean using words (when reading, writing, listening, speaking, or conversing) or other meaning carriers such as images, art, music, and movement. Meaningful things include making decisions, solving problems, changing minds, and building up valuable ideas. And one or more other people are needed because they provide or have a need for new or different information.

There are three features that form the backbone of authentic communication in a learning activity. The activity should require and help students do the following three things: (1) purposefully build one or more ideas, (2) clarify and support ideas, and (3) fill information gaps.

These three features are vital not only for talking and listening but also for reading, writing, conversing, viewing, composing, and dramatizing. One of the main purposes of the following chapters is to help you enhance teaching activities in ways that strengthen these three features as much as possible.

FEATURE 1: REQUIRES AND HELPS STUDENTS TO PURPOSEFULLY BUILD ONE OR MORE IDEAS

The first and most important feature of authentic communication is the purposeful building of one or more ideas. An idea is any concept, hypothesis, conclusion, story, theory, solution, or other abstract construct that can be built up with smaller things such as examples and clarifications. I can often tell if a response is an idea when a student says a sentence and I want the student to say more by clarifying or supporting it with examples. For example, if a student says, "Animals use energy to grow, heal, and keep warm," I want some clarification of what it means to use energy and I want some animal examples. Or if a student raises her hand and says, "We need to appreciate how people are different," I would like to hear evidence for this idea that she found in the text or in life. I want to know how the text's examples support or clarify the idea that she is building about respecting and celebrating the many ways in which people and groups of people are different—an idea that she will hopefully continue to build throughout her life. Here are some other ideas:

- The energy that animals have originated from the sun.
- I think we should all be more like Montag, even if we lose everything we have.
- When you split a number up into equal parts, you divide.
- Brian became more independent out in the wilderness.
- I can use the story of when I moved here to show the theme of overcoming fears.

- You need to think about bias when using primary sources in history.

- All life needs water.

- I say we come up with two equations with the same two variables.

- Geography influences the beliefs and customs of people who live in it.

- Multiplying fractions makes them even smaller.

- I can use a baseball bat, baseball, and a car to show Newton's three laws.

- The European explorers were motivated mostly by greed.

As you can see, ideas come in a variety of types. Some ideas solve problems and help you be a better person; others inform, convince, deepen understandings, define, and inspire. Ideas also come in various "sizes." For example, the idea "Bias has influenced the documenting of history over time" is more on the large side, while the idea "The use of the term *Boston Massacre* was a way to get colonists angrier" would be more on the medium side. "Gravity plays a large role in forming galaxies and planetary systems" is a large idea, while "When the distance between two objects increases, the gravitational forces between them decrease" might be a more medium-sized idea.

Bigger ideas are often built up with smaller ideas and "bricks," such as evidence, clarifications, examples, facts, details, questions, answers, fixed misconceptions, and so on. These bricks often come from past experiences, conversations, reading, writing, listening, watching, and reflecting. Here is a visual that roughly shows a partially built-up idea.

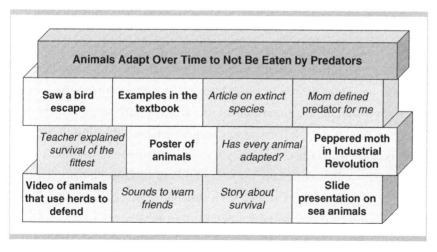

Figure 1.1   Model of Reina's Partial Building of an Idea in Fourth-Grade Science

As you can see in this partially constructed idea, a lot of different bricks are used from a student's past and present. In this model, the *teal* bricks mostly fall in the clarifying category and the **gray** ones tend to include evidence and examples that support the idea. These differences are not always clear, though. For example, an example might be used to clarify, and a clarification is often needed in order to explain how evidence supports an idea. If it's useful for building, I usually don't care what color it is.

Many larger ideas are built over time. Ideas can last for decades and even entire lifetimes. You and I are still building up, reinforcing, and even tearing down and changing ideas that got their start in K–12 lessons. And many of the bigger ideas are made of medium and small ideas, like the sample shown in Figure 1.2.

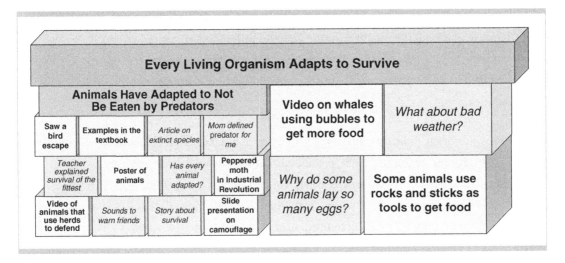

Figure 1.2   Model of Reina's Use of the Idea from Figure 1.1 to Build Up an Even Bigger Idea

Just as students differ, so do the ways in which they build up ideas. One student will have read or seen or heard things that another student hasn't read or seen or heard. In fact, when students are given opportunities to share their ideas with one another, it is even more helpful to have differently constructed ideas, because when they share, they further strengthen one another's ideas. Two students might both have the idea that Rosa Parks was a hero, but they might have read different stories, seen different video clips, had conversations with different people, remember different details, value different traits of heroes, and emphasize different events. When they meet and share these bricks, their ideas become bigger and stronger.

This type of building is very different from the standardized "all students must memorize these facts and build up ideas in the same exact way" view of learning. It is more complex and messier than the models of knowledge construction often represented by lists and outlines (e.g., sets of standards). There are two key aspects of this feature: (1) building ideas is purposeful, and (2) there is some meaningful change, growth, or difference.

Building ideas is purposeful. This means that students do something meaningful with the ideas that they build. It can be real-world or not. But the motivation to communicate must go beyond rewards, praise, or pleasing the teacher. It should even go beyond just building up an idea. Purposeful and engaging ideas include preparing a TED Talk, transforming a story into a play, interpreting a graph, arguing to spend money on jaguar conservation, deciding how to design a model of our galaxy, clarifying an opinion about a hot topic, and coming up with a way to solve a certain type of math problem.

There is some meaningful change, growth, or difference. It occurs in the minds or hearts of students when they build up ideas. The idea should endure beyond a particular lesson or unit. For example, if a student learns about ant colonies in second grade, this idea of insects and other living things living in colonies, playing different roles, etc., can and should last and grow for years. Or with respect to the heart, a student might read about the many children in other countries who need to work in dangerous jobs to feed their families. The student then decides to address the problem by raising money for a child sponsorship program.

This feature is essential for authentic communication because it gives students an engaging, challenging, and rewarding reason to think and use language. Building ideas fulfills their minds' yearning to create, solve, and evolve. It also provides coherence that the mind needs for long-term retention of new content and language.

FEATURE 2: REQUIRES AND HELPS STUDENTS TO CLARIFY AND SUPPORT

Every activity should require and help students to clarify and support ideas. These are the two main skills used for building up an idea. Even though clarifying and supporting overlap quite a bit, clarifying tends to mean using language and other cues to help a reader, listener, or viewer to understand something.

And supporting means using accurate content and evidence to strengthen the truth, justification, completeness, or value of an idea. For example, you might tell students, in pairs, to prepare a presentation about how different types of energy transform. They need to create a poster that clearly shows strong examples of transformations with solid and correct explanations of how they work. Students also need to organize the presentation in a clear order, use words and expressions that the poster's viewers will understand, and be ready to clarify the terms. They might then work on their clarity by practicing the presentation in front of another pair, getting feedback on how clear it is, and then presenting to a different group.

Clarity and support need to be needed for accomplishing the task or being successful in the activity. If they aren't required, then students are less likely to put forth the effort to make ideas clear and strong for others—or for themselves. It's a lot of work to clarify and support ideas. If a student doesn't feel that the information that she is sharing or receiving is needed, then she will likely not take the time or effort to clarify or support. And I'm not just picking on students here; we adults do the same—and often worse.

When an activity *requires* clarifying and supporting, it causes students to push themselves and push their peers for clarity and support. This is helpful because many students still need to learn (a) what it means to learn through building up ideas and (b) that it takes more clarifying and supporting than what they usually think is needed. This is yet another place where you, the teacher, comes in. You will need to intentionally push students to push themselves and others to use these skills. Often you will need to put this pushing into an activity's procedures, into your teaching practices, and into fostering student habits of how they interact and learn. Of course, the activity should be engaging and purposeful enough (see Feature 1) for students to want to put the extra effort into building, changing, clarifying, and supporting.

You will notice that many of the enhanced activities in later chapters include a requirement that students ask a clarifying question ("What do you mean by...?") or a supporting question ("Why...?") when they are reading, writing, listening, speaking, conversing, etc. Yes, I realize that pushing students to ask such questions isn't 100 percent authentic because they might not feel that they need clarification or support. But they often do—more than they think. And the ultimate results of them developing these habits and seeing much more clarity and support are worth it.

FEATURE 3: REQUIRES AND HELPS STUDENTS TO FILL INFORMATION GAPS

A learning activity should have information gaps that students need to fill in order to accomplish the task. An information gap exists when one person has information that the other person doesn't have but needs or wants in order to accomplish a task or satisfy an interest. If I want to learn more about what drove Leonardo da Vinci to be so creative, I might read an article on him that was written by an expert. Through my reading of the article, the author authentically communicates to me, filling certain information gaps. Then if I talk to a friend who watched a documentary on da Vinci, she tells me more information that I didn't know that helps me build up my idea of what fueled his creativity. I could then listen to podcasts, tell an interested friend my idea, have a back-and-forth conversation with a different friend, and even write my own article that will be read by people interested in the topic. My talking, conversing, and writing about my idea help me to build it up and, as a bonus, they help my friends to build up their ideas on the topic.

Lessons can offer rich opportunities to fill information gaps. Students differ widely with respect to backgrounds, homes, experiences, books they have read, shows they have watched, articles and social media comments they have read, images they have seen, and so on. They have learned and remember different things. They build up ideas in different ways and have a wide range of values, interests, and opinions. As we think of designing activities and tasks for lessons, we can take advantage of the rich variety of gaps that can be bridged.

Then again, many students who are with each other most of the school day have read the same texts, seen the same videos, and encountered the same lessons. Often, the teacher needs to intentionally provide different information to different students and set up the activity so that students need to share the information with each other. A common example is a jigsaw activity in which different small groups of students read different texts or portions of a text, becoming "experts" who share their information with others who didn't read their text. But jigsaws alone are not enough to spark authentic communication. In the following chapters we will look at how to enhance jigsaws and many other activities in order to create and leverage information gaps.

As you observe students engaging in activities with authentic communication, you will notice some struggling to express their thoughts and form their questions. Productive struggle is good, but if a student is struggling so much to communicate that he or she gives up, then the task is not authentic and not helpful. Such students can benefit from language scaffolds such as modeling, using sentence starters, getting extra practice, and using formative feedback.

Language scaffolding should serve one, two, or all three features of authentic communication. Does the support help students to build up ideas? Does it help students to support or clarify? Does it help them bridge information gaps? A common strategy in many classrooms is having students use sentence starters and frames. Yet these shouldn't just be terms or phrases that we use to teach students "academic" language. If it doesn't scaffold one or more of the three features, then we shouldn't use it. The language likely won't stick very well in students' minds.

CONCLUSION

Our brains yearn to learn through authentic communication. And yet, much of the communication in school isn't authentic, especially in Grades 3 through 12. I have heard a range of reasons for this lack of authenticity, such as "This is how I was taught. It won't raise test scores. It's too hard to assess. It's too loud. It's too much work. The curriculum doesn't have it. This is what we do in school." We need to move beyond excuses like these to see the potential for deeper learning through more authentic communication.

REFLECTION QUESTIONS

1. Have your ideas about teaching and learning changed by reading this chapter? How?

2. What tends to be pseudo-communication and authentic communication in your classroom?

3. How might more authentic communication influence learning in your setting?

CULTIVATING A CLASSROOM CULTURE OF COMMUNICATION

Were all instructors to realize that the quality of mental process, not the production of correct answers, is the measure of educative growth, something hardly less than a revolution in teaching would be worked.

—John Dewey

Classroom culture plays a huge role in fostering authentic communication. Culture, in a nutshell, is how people do things in any given setting. In a classroom, this includes what teachers and students do, what they say, what they value, how they relate to one another, and even how they think. So, for a classroom culture of communication, this means improving how teachers and students communicate to facilitate learning and growth. It includes how we choose to teach, design lessons and activities, make adjustments during lessons, assess learning, and help students to interact and build relationships. It also includes how we develop and leverage students' values, attitudes, and beliefs about how to learn and communicate.

First, teachers and students need to have enough overlap in their views of what it means to learn in school. For example, *you* might understand the importance of communication, but your students might not. Putting up a façade of authentic communication onto your students' framework of pseudo-communication won't work. If students expect points for everything they do in class and you say to them, "Now we are going to communicate with one another without focusing on points," student learning will be less robust. The reverse is also true. If your students want and expect to communicate, but you are focused on coverage, transmission of information, and having students do things for points, their learning will be less substantial.

You have likely seen and used a variety of classroom posters with norms for behavior and classroom culture. Many posters include things such as *Respect each other, Be responsible, Assume good intentions,* and so on. These can be helpful, but on their own they tend to be too generic, static, and ignored to foster the type of classroom culture needed for authentic communication. Fostering a safe and rich culture for communicating requires a commitment to five fairly big elements that work together for authenticity: (1) fostering engaged learning, (2) cultivating idea-building mindsets, (3) fostering student agency and ownership of learning, (4) developing skills in order to build up ideas, and (5) knowing your students' communication strengths and needs.

FOSTER ENGAGED LEARNING

Let's start with the most important element in cultivating a culture of authentic communication: engagement. Engagement is the degree to which a student is intrinsically interested or motivated to do something, such as learning a topic, participating in a learning activity, doing an assessment, making a difference, or communicating with others about important things. It tends to refer to the amount or intensity of the curiosity, attention, creativity, motivation, and passion that students feel as they do something. Students who are engaged tend to keep thinking about the learning even when they don't have to. They persevere in spite of obstacles and setbacks, and they see themselves progressing toward some worthy goal(s). These aspects of engagement help to enrich authentic communication and vice versa.

Yet the engagement challenge is enormous. First of all, we have a wide range of students. It's hard for teachers to make everything interesting for all 34 (or in some cases, 164) students. Second, with a wide range of other interesting things competing for students' interest (e.g., video games, social media, movies), things like academic skills, content concepts, and standards often fail to hook students into learning at deep levels. Third, the writers of most sets of standards did not make student engagement a priority. Fourth, many of the curriculums that we are supposed to use are a few bricks short of interesting. They are trying to cover their standards bases, and they have difficulty motivating and connecting to the needs of diverse students.

Here are several ways to increase engagement in order to strengthen learning through authentic communication.

Choose interesting topics. Some students, for example, get quite engaged in the challenge of building a robot that needs to do a task on Mars, while others might get hooked into the controversy of whether or not cell phone use should be allowed in class. At times we can choose the topic or text based on what interests students. Choice is more common in English language arts (ELA) and English language development (ELD) classes, but there are ways to emphasize certain topics in other classes, depending on the interests of students. If, for example, you are teaching about European exploration and colonization, you can give students choices of specific explorers or events to research in order to write an argument-based article or create a presentation.

Create engaging tasks and activities. Some students will engage in learning about a topic that doesn't interest them if the learning task is interesting, engaging, and/or social. Some will more likely write an argument in an article than in an essay to the teacher (How many people in the world get excited about writing or even reading essays?). Other students like doing posters, computer-based projects, dramatizations, and presentations in which they teach something to others. In one class that I observed, students were trying to decide which route to California in the mid-1800s was better for the roles they had been given. They needed to do some reading, writing, and arguing with others. Some weren't interested in the topic, per se, but they got engaged in the task and its procedures.

Challenge students. Some students like to overcome interesting challenges and problems. These might include solving complex math or physics problems, performing science labs, using primary sources to answer a big history question, interpreting a song, etc. The actual topic is usually of interest, but it might not be, and the students' focus is really on the challenge. When the challenge requires communication with others for success, even better. When a student thinks, "I want to overcome this challenge but I know I need to read, listen, and discuss with others to accomplish the task," engagement and communication increase.

Make learning useful. Engagement can also relate to how much a student perceives the learning to be useful—now or in the future. If a student sees the topic or skill as being important for short- or long-term future success—even though it might not seem useful at the moment—then its motivational value tends to increase (Husman & Lens, 1999). While it is very hard to have everything we do in every lesson be directly connected to the real world, we can often make it a bit more like the real world. We can assign roles and create tasks that at least have some logical connections and potential for use in the real world, such as the following:

- History students compare primary sources to create a letter to a textbook company that proposes major content changes in a chapter.

- Science students solve a local water pollution problem by first measuring the levels of pollution in the water and then putting together a report and video presentation for the local government.

- Math students figure out costs of materials and labor for a school renovation project or put together a business proposal for a student-run company.

- English students write poems to inform people about injustices in their community.

- In government class, a mock Congress might appeal to students who want to learn how the federal legislative branch works.

Use drama. An important yet often neglected component of engagement is drama. Drama is the process of tapping into our natural fascinations with life's many types of stories and situations. Humans tend to value the plot-like dimensions of life such as characters, conflict, unexpected twists in the action, exciting resolutions, and the lessons learned throughout a story. Humans are drawn to drama because we can identify with characters and we can experience vicarious emotions and lessons that our daily lives don't always offer. One study showed that the use of elements such as make-believe, role-playing, exaggeration, and imagination during instruction increases student interest in learning (see Pintrich, 2001). Students like to be involved, be creative, use their imaginations, improvise, and be engaged in a story as they learn. For example, students and/or teachers can act like characters in a novel, heroes, villains, soldiers, planets, atoms, revolutionaries, presidents, etc. Students might balance the federal budget, stage an archaeological dig, act out a modern-day version of *The Odyssey*, or use a science fiction film to show astronomy principles.

Make learning worth the energy. One factor that reduces students' engagement is when they determine that the costs in terms of time, energy, and psychological risks (e.g., embarrassment) of doing any particular activity are not worth the potential benefits (Wigfield & Eccles, 1992). If benefits outweigh the costs, then interest increases. For example, if the large amount of reading and writing about a topic of moderate interest seems to be worth the final product of creating a website that is accessed by the entire school or beyond, then engagement might increase. But if the reading and writing is just to pass a test, the costs might outweigh the benefits of a few extra points. Because authentic communication-based learning is focused on building up important ideas that students deem to be valuable beyond Friday's quiz, it often engages students more.

We want to create situations in which students' motivation to communicate reaches and exceeds their "it's worth the energy" threshold. We sometimes forget that communication takes a lot of energy. We can't just assume that students will communicate (read, write, listen, speak, converse) just because they are in school or because they will get a few points. Imagine two students who are in a group working on creating a simple robot. Lisa doesn't care about robots but does care about points. Amir likes robots and doesn't care about points. Amir reads a short article—twice— about robots because he wants to figure out how to make the robot move. Lisa reads it once because the teacher asked her to. A lot more learning will likely stick in Amir's mind.

Shift the focus from getting points to learning. Many students have developed their skills for "playing school." They have learned to keep quiet, turn in their work, minimally answer questions, talk as little as possible in class and group discussions, and stay out of trouble year after year. Too many students do this. They learn much less than what they could learn because they do just enough to get by rather than put the extra mental effort into building and communicating lasting ideas. And it's not their fault! We must strive to do away with the game playing and instead build a culture in the classroom that focuses on engaged learning. This doesn't mean we need to get rid of points and grades. We can still assess learning and assign grades, but, as much as possible, these shouldn't be the main motivation in students' minds. The content, the ideas, the thinking, the tasks, and the communication should be the top priorities.

I know many teachers, mostly in secondary settings, who express concern when I bring up this suggestion. Some have said things such as "You think that without giving them points my students are just going to light up from the sheer joy of solving quadratic equations, reading *The Federalist Papers*, writing five-paragraph essays, or taking science tests? No way." Even though the points-based system can work in some settings for some students, I have seen too many classrooms in which the students we are most concerned about are the least motivated by grades. If we put all of our motivation-engagement eggs into the grades and points basket, many students will continue to get low grades, slide by, do the bare minimum, and not learn enough. This should be reason enough to try some of the suggestions in this book.

In one middle school math class the teacher began the year explaining a poster with a mantra: "Building ideas is first; getting points is second!" She told students that they would design a scale model of the school in order to learn about ratios. The students needed to use the scale model and sample problems to construct key mathematical ideas, and they had to convince her and others that they knew the ideas well. They would also get points for these products and presentations, but the points were a secondary focus. This teacher worked within the current system of giving points and letter grades, but she did not let the system get in the way of rich learning. She didn't just rely on the threat of low grades to motivate learning.

Another teacher I know gives points for building up ideas. She codeveloped a checklist tool for students to use in order to remind them of what is needed to robustly, clearly, and completely build up ideas. Students also used a visual similar to the idea-building blueprint visuals that are introduced in this chapter (see Figure 2.2 later in the chapter or the online appendix). Students in her class said that it is highly motivating to get deep into learning and building up a new idea—and then get points for it as a bonus! One student even said it was like getting paid to eat ice cream.

Sure, most students will be bored at times in school, and no student will be engaged all the time, but we can do much more in the average school day, especially for the students who tend to do the bare minimum. For many students it's not enough to just be motivated to learn things. They also need to be motivated to communicate and be communicated to during the learning. For these students, communication is the necessary catalyst that clarifies the learning, deepens it, and makes it stick.

This and several other parts of this book might suggest that I am arguing for abolishing tests, points, and grades. I'm not. I am arguing that tests (particularly the ones with lots of random multiple-choice and short-answer questions) should not be the culmination of, the motivation for, nor the goal of learning. Tests and quizzes should be auxiliary tools used to provide an extra window into what students have learned and need to learn to build up ideas. For example, I heard a teacher say something like "I don't want you to study for the quiz; I want you to study to improve your knowledge to help you on your performance task. I will use the quiz to see if there are any needs that I should address in upcoming lessons."

CULTIVATE IDEA-BUILDING MINDSETS IN STUDENTS

Do you ever wonder what students are thinking during a lesson? Often I get the sense that their focus is on quickly completing whatever activity they are doing. Perhaps some are assuming they will learn something from it and, if not, they will at least get credit in the form of points or a grade for having done something. And, while it is tempting to rely on engagement and motivation, they are not enough. For effective idea building to happen in our classrooms, we need to encourage a change in student mindsets about learning.

First of all, we need to convince students of the importance of building up ideas. Second, we need to teach them how to build up ideas (see Chapter 1). Third, we want students to be on the lookout ("read-out" and "listen-out") for ideas to build every day in school. Fourth, we want students to develop the mental habit of asking the four questions in Figure 2.1. The questions embody four mindsets that help students to build ideas in school and in life.

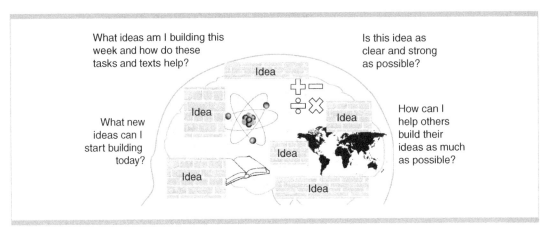

Figure 2.1　Sample Anchor Chart for Questions Based on Four Idea-Building Mindsets

Mindset 1: I'm on the Lookout for New Ideas to Build

The first mindset is focused on student openness and readiness for building up ideas. If they know that in this classroom they are supposed to build ideas in order to learn, then they are more likely to see how the lesson activities help them do this building. If they don't have this mindset, then they likely just have a "What do I have to do today?" mindset, which tends to be surface level and temporary learning. Of course, teachers must help students get excited about posing and choosing new ideas to build up. Teachers often have students share their beginning ideas with others to show the class the importance of this mindset. In other words, we need to make students aware that this is a central purpose of every activity. We need to talk to them about its importance overall and in relationship to specific tasks, and we must help them become more aware of themselves as idea builders.

Mindset 2: I Try to Use All That We Do in Class to Build Up Ideas

This mindset gives a purpose for the knowledge and skills learned across a variety of activities, lessons, and units that we use to teach. For example, a fifth grader with this mindset might start the history lesson thinking, "Yesterday, I started to build up my idea about how the early colonists survived with the help of Wampanoag people. What are we doing today that helps me build my idea up more?" And when the first activity begins, such as a jigsaw reading, the student thinks, "Okay, now I am going to add to my idea with my reading and with the information shared by my peers." When appropriate, teachers can share the ideas that they intend for students to learn in a unit and then explicitly share how the lessons and activities will help students to build them up.

It can help to use the idea-building blueprint (see Figure 2.2) or similar graphic organizer that keeps track of the "building blocks" that are used to build up the key ideas. In the general blueprint, students put notes that build up the central idea in the blocks (boxes) below it. The larger blocks are for more important evidence and clarifications. For the math blueprint, students put mathematical principles, properties, and definitions in some blocks and sample problems in other blocks. Chapters 3 through 7 refer to these visual organizers often.

Mindset 3: I Work Hard to Make My Ideas as Clear, Strong, and Complete as Possible

Imagine, after asking a question to the class, all of your students think, "My answer needs to be as clear, strong, and complete as possible. Let me think about how to do this so that no person listening to me (or reading my writing) needs to ask me to clarify or support it. I will have already done this for them." It sounds pie in the sky, but it is possible. And this mindset of making one's message as clear, strong, and as complete as possible will be helpful in the future when students can't depend on teachers or parents to keep prompting them to do and say more.

If students don't have this mindset of pushing themselves to support ideas and be understood as well as possible, over the long haul there is less thinking, language using, and learning. Consider any activity that you use in your classroom, and think about whether it provides enough engagement and purpose for students say to themselves, "It's worth trying to strengthen my response, so I'll add evidence to it when I say it again" or "I will ask my partner to clarify because I really want to know what she means, and what she says will add to my idea."

Mindset 4: I Want to Help Others Build Their Ideas as Much as Possible

Each classroom is a learning community, and the more that we can emphasize the *community* aspects, the better. This mindset helps students to be less self-centered and less competitive with respect to learning. Remind students that we can learn a lot more and better when we work together and support one

Idea-Building Blueprint—General

IDEA (Key Concept, Claim, Answer to Essential Question, etc.) in my own words:

Why it's important:

How this connects to or depends on other ideas:

Real-world applications (if any):

Visual Ways to Represent and Remember This Idea (symbols, drawings, etc.)

(Clarification)	(Reason)	Evidence	(Clarification)
(Example)			
( )	( )	( )	( )
( )	( )	( )	( )
( )	( )	( )	( )

Idea-Building Blueprint—Math

IDEA (Key Concept; Standard; Answer to Essential Question) in my own words:

Why it's important:

How this connects to or depends on other ideas:

Real-world applications (if any):

Visual Ways to Represent and Remember This Idea (symbols, drawings, graphs, etc.)

Principle, Property, Theorem, Definition	Principle, Property, Theorem, Definition
Sample Problem ❏ Given to me ❏ Found by me ❏ Created by me/us)	**Sample Problem** ❏ Given to me ❏ Found by me ❏ Created by me or us)
How this problem supports or shows the big ideas	How this problem supports or shows the big ideas
Sample Problem ❏ Given to me ❏ Found by me ❏ Created by me or us)	**Sample Problem** ❏ Given to me ❏ Found by me ❏ Created by me or us)
How this problem supports or shows the big ideas	How this problem supports or shows the big ideas

Figure 2.2 Idea-Building Blueprints (General and Math)

Full-sized versions of these blueprints available for download at **resources.corwin.com/CommunicationEffect**

another in learning activities. And communication is more authentic when students think that what they are saying and writing is making an impact on others. Enhanced think-pair-shares (see Chapters 4 and 5) and Stronger and Clearer Each Time activities (see Chapter 5) are examples of activities that encourage students to help others build ideas. I suggest that teachers highlight the importance of helping others build ideas as often as they can during lessons.

FOSTER STUDENT AGENCY AND OWNERSHIP OF LEARNING

Rather than just providing *access* to the "warehouses" of knowledge and skills, we should want students to *own* the warehouses and then use what's in them to build up other buildings. This means that we set up opportunities for students to use knowledge and skills so that they own rather than just "borrow" them for a short amount of time. Agency means that students feel that they have some real control over what they are thinking and building in their minds. That's why Feature 1 (see Chapter 1) of authentic communication is so important. Students will build up ideas in different ways, and they know this. This makes it more powerful because (a) a student's way of constructing an idea isn't wrong compared to the ideas of teachers or peers, and (b) students tend to push themselves to clarify it and support it because they own the idea as opposed to just memorizing it.

Most people in the world, young and old, want to have some control over what they learn and how they learn it. Yet for too many students, schooling has given them the sense that whatever they do and how hard they work won't make enough of a difference. When students do gain some control over their learning experiences, their "buy-in" and motivation to learn increase (see Stipek, 2002). For example, in previous years, an eighth-grade history teacher had all students write essays on the causes of the westward expansion. This year he had students choose two motivations for moving west and argue for one of them in an advertisement they designed for potential pioneers. Students had some choice and control in the process as well as the chance to be creative, which fed their feelings of agency and engagement.

Nurture Student Voice

Students need to feel that (a) they can share their perspectives, their solutions to problems, and their interpretations, and (b) these are needed and valued by others for learning. Students are motivated to learn when they think things such as "My teacher and my classmates are interested in what I have to say, and my ideas are useful to them, their idea building, and their growth as people." Like many of the elements in this chapter, there is a bit of "chicken or egg" going on: providing opportunities for students to voice their ideas fosters authentic communication, and authentic communication activities tend to encourage students to voice their ideas. You will see many examples in the following chapters of students voicing their ideas in ways that enrich learning.

Let Students Have More Control

"I don't know what they are saying or thinking back there" is a common worry when teachers allow students to talk to each other. Yet to have a classroom that values authentic communication, the teacher must be willing to give up more control than what may feel comfortable. When you give up some control, at times students might not be talking about or thinking about the particular standard that we had in mind for this lesson. But they might learn something related, break new mental ground, or sow healthy seeds for learning future standards. They might even reinforce their learning of standards that were covered several months ago.

As students gain more agency and control over what and how they are learning, not only do they communicate more but they *want* to communicate more. I remember a fifth grader who had done very little reading or writing because I had been giving a lot of typical reading and writing assignments (e.g., "Respond to this story and answer the questions."). Then I told the class that they needed to choose a story with an important topic connected to the American Revolution and read up on the topic in order to create a historical fiction short story from the point of view of someone during that time. A week later he turned in a fascinating twenty-two-page story draft, handwritten.

Often, we need to trust the process and let authentic communication do the work. Yes, some of the learning may be invisible. This includes facts, ideas, and skills that start or continue to grow in students' minds but are not visible on the quizzes, tests, or year-end exams. But invisible learning is okay. Some of the most important and lasting things that humans learn take time to develop, and we may never figure out how to assess them in a manner that produces neat and clean numbers on spreadsheets.

Cultivate Student Creativity

There are plenty of articles and lectures that you can listen to that describe the lack of student creativity in our teaching and curriculums. Creativity is hard to test and therefore rare in curriculum materials that are written to prepare students for year-end tests. And yet, being creative tends to be one of the top three traits that employers are looking for. (Note: Numbers one and two are often things like collaboration and communication, which you will also find aplenty in this book.)

Creativity means using innovative thinking to meet challenges and express ideas. It includes finding new solutions to new and old problems. And problems abound. Many are getting worse. Just look at environmental problems, political divides, war, social issues, poverty, and so on. When students graduate, they need to be the most creative people who ever lived. But is current schooling helping to build their creativity skills? Writing a personal narrative in ELA a few times per year (to prepare for a writing assessment) is not enough. We need to improve creativity development in every grade level and every subject area.

How does creativity foster communication and vice versa? First of all, it helps students to build confidence and a sense of agency, mentioned previously, because tasks that call for creativity tend to also be those that give students control over how or what they are learning. There also tends to be a lot of emotional investment that comes from expressing oneself. Students might be asked to create a lab to understand water pollution, a poster to argue a certain historical point of view, a math problem, a short story, a website, etc. As they create, they build up ideas in unique ways. (In Chapter 8, we will spend time on what it means to use teacher creativity to overcome the challenges of making communication more authentic in our schools.)

DEVELOP SKILLS IN ORDER TO BUILD IDEAS

In recent decades there have been many efforts, lists, standards, and curriculums that have focused on developing important academic and life skills. These often include collaborating, problem solving, using creativity, and critical thinking. Thinking skills that tend to fall into these four categories include analyzing, interpreting, inferring, taking multiple perspectives, arguing, identifying causes and effects, evaluating, and comparing. These skills are highly useful across a wide range of topics and subject areas now and in the future.

Yet often the skills are taught and tested in isolation. Teachers teach the skills because they are on a list of objectives or standards, in order to "cover" them. They develop much better when they are taught in the context of building up core ideas in a discipline. It is a bit analogous to developing construction skills in the real world. You can learn to measure, saw, and hammer with scrap pieces of wood in a garage. But when you use the skills to build a real house, they matter a lot more, you get to see the direct results of using them, and they last a lot longer.

Some standards, for example, tell students to compare and contrast characters in a novel or two historical events, etc. Yet if I am a student, I would ask, "Why should I compare these two things?" If it's just to "develop the skill of comparing" because some standard tells me to, I won't work very hard on it. But if you tell me that comparing the two characters will help me craft my own stories or develop insights into people, myself, and life, then I see more purpose and I am more likely to work harder.

Our goal should be to frame skill development so that if we ask students why they are working on a certain skill, they can answer, "This skill helps me to build up the idea of ... in this way..." For example, as students are learning to infer biases in primary sources, instead of the student saying, "We are learning this skill because it's on the test," we should want them to say something like "We are learning the skill of inferring bias in sources because it helps us to build up more complete ideas about what really happened in history and why. Every source has bias. For example, ..." Or in math, we would like students to say, "We are learning the skill of dividing fractions because in life we will sometimes need to know how many fractions fit inside other fractions, and we will need to this for solving more advanced problems in math, science, and the business world. For example, ..."

KNOW YOUR STUDENTS' COMMUNICATION STRENGTHS AND NEEDS

You have often heard of the importance of getting to know your students, which is both vital and challenging. In this section, I zoom in on getting to know our students' communication strengths and needs. This is important because different students (and groups of students) have a wide range of communication styles, abilities, preferences, and resources. Here are few practical suggestions for getting to know these things.

Formatively Assess Communication Skills

Many curriculums have been designed to produce higher scores on once-a-year machine-scored tests. And many people inside and outside of education tend to judge instructional approaches, strategies, curriculums, and teachers on how well their students do on the tests. As a researcher, a question that I often ask teachers is "How do you know this approach works?" Even large research studies that look at instructional interventions and approaches tend to use test scores and written products as measures of effectiveness. And yet we also need to assess students' abilities to speak, listen, converse, collaborate, and write to inform readers who want and need the information. We need to assess their abilities to read literature and nonfiction texts for the reasons they were written. We need to assess students' empathy, creativity, and tenacity. And I'm sure that you have a list of additional highly important things that the big year-end tests don't assess.

Have you had any students who show their learning later than the pacing guides dictate? Do your assessments (e.g., standardized tests, benchmark exams, quizzes, essays) fail to effectively assess communication? It is an art to communicate as clearly and strongly as possible—and often differently—to, from, and with different people. We need to keep working on the use of portfolios, performance assessments, big projects, presentations that matter, audio-recorded messages, and other ways that allow students—not force them— to show what they have learned. All of these, of course, take more time and energy than the common bubble-in test.

Every activity, including any written or recorded products, gives you a chance to see how students are using language and other means to communicate. Formative assessment practices include the use of strategies and tools for observing, questioning, and reflecting on the effectiveness of student communication. In many of the enhanced activities in the following chapters, students are taking notes, filling in visual organizers, writing, and recording their ideas orally. You can use all of these, along with observations and reflection conferences with students, to assess their communication abilities.

Strengthen the Signs of Authentic Communication

The three features of authentic communication are not that easy to see, but it helps to be on the lookout for the more visible signs. Here are the main ones.

Students "productively struggle" to communicate. It's gold when you see a student genuinely try to communicate. At that moment, you are seeing learning; you are seeing the student push herself to build up an idea for others—and for herself. A related look-for is positive mental exhaustion—in students, not you. I was observing a high school lesson that had focused on speaking and listening to build up academic ideas. Afterward, a student said, "Wow, I never used my brain that much in school before!"

Students consider right answers to be the beginning of learning, not the end of it. Right answers, especially the short ones, can and should become seeds or building blocks for more robust and complete concepts and understandings. For example, the typical student in math tends to try to get the right answer to a problem as quickly as possible. But if you give him the right answer from the start—and then prompt the student to strive to communicate, as clearly as possible, the procedures and reasoning that resulted in that answer—then his learning will likely increase.

Students draw out, encourage, and support the language use of other students. This means that students act like teachers, in a sense, as they push others to make their ideas as clear and strong as possible. Students ask teacher-esque questions such as "What do you mean by...? Can you clarify... Can you give a couple examples of that?" The more a student feels that her ideas are valuable and needed by other students, the more focused thinking and language the student is likely to use.

Students are engaged in long-term and short-term projects. These include project-based learning or problem-based learning (PBL), or variations of these. PBL usually gives students a chance to engage in deeper uses of language and content ideas because they are focused on building up an idea or solution that wasn't there before. Feature 1 in this book, Purposeful building of ideas (see Chapter 1) is part of the fabric of the approach. As students work to complete their projects, they build up robust idea(s) and skills over time, often working with others to reinforce key aspects of learning. Usually there is some choice of topic, a choice of how to approach the learning, and a choice of how to communicate the final product(s) to others. One teacher I know mentioned that one of her former students remembered the ideas and even some details from a project that he had done in her class several years before.

Use Norms, Mantras, and Mottos That Foster Communication

Hopefully this chapter has given you some ideas about cultivating a communication-based classroom culture, and perhaps you have even taken some notes that you could turn into norms, mantras, and mottos. Take some time to get to know what your students need, and then work with them to develop these. You can even think about icons or images to go with them. I included some examples here to give you an idea of what some teachers have used. Feel free to take them, change them, add to them, or even sell them if you can find a buyer.

In this classroom, we do the following:

- Always be on the lookout for interesting and important ideas to build up.
- Build up ideas as much as we can by clarifying and supporting them.
- Build up the first idea first.
- Don't popcorn out ideas (unless it is brainstorming that we do on purpose to choose ideas to build up).
- Listen super attentively to others in order to build up ideas.
- Park our opinions in the back of our minds until we have built up all ideas as much as possible.
- Collaboratively build up competing ideas in an argument with equal effort.
- Don't be happy with minimal responses from peers.
- Don't be happy with our own minimal responses.
- Help and push each other to be as clear and strong as possible.
- Support ideas with the best examples, evidence, and reasons that we can find.
- Value the ideas of others and think about how to use them.
- Have the following priorities: first, helping others to build ideas; second, helping ourselves build ideas; and third, developing friendships and collaboration skills.

Cultivate Relationships

One of the most important parts of being human is our relationships with others. Our students need to know how to build and maintain relationships such as friendships with a wide range of others throughout life. We don't see much about relationships in standards and assessments, but they are vital for communication-based learning. The topic of friendship, for example, often emerges when looking at both fiction and nonfiction stories. This is a great place to talk about what it means to be a friend and how to start friendships with others who are different from us. Yet all content classes should also work to foster friendships. Often this is done in pair and small-group activities—many of which are in this book.

In addition to the content-focused objectives for a lesson or activity, you can look for relationship qualities or social skills objectives that your students need to work on. Examples include being patient; forgiving others; sacrificing; valuing others' ideas; not making fun of others; wanting the best for your friends; trusting others; and being trustworthy, honest, loyal, empathetic, and nonjudgmental. Look for instances in student interactions that you can (a) highlight and reinforce these qualities and actions ("Great job showing empathy for your partner!") and (b) help students improve them ("Remember not to judge or criticize your partner.").

Now take a moment to reflect how vital these soft skills and qualities are—not just for individuals but also for communities and societies. We often need to remind ourselves that our work with students is meant to develop them well beyond what is required in common curriculums, standards, and assessments.

Scaffold Language Needed for Communication

We need to get to know our students' language needs and use that information to set them up for rich communication. And then we must give them the freedom to communicate, no matter how messy it becomes. Here are some specific suggestions for doing this, some of which might seem counterintuitive.

Strive for messiness. The challenge of engaging in this kind of learning, especially for those who like everything to be neat and ordered and "aligned," is that the more authentic communication there is, the messier the learning tends to be. We might even call it productive messiness, which means that (a) not every student learns the same content and language in each activity and (b) you (the teacher) cannot know all of the language and content that students learn during the activity.

Don't overfocus on language development. Language development tends to grow more when it is not the focus. This may seem odd when you think of all the language education books and computer programs, but remember the power of being immersed in meaningful language use at home as a child (first language acquisition) or of moving to another country and immersing oneself in using the new language (second language acquisition) to get things done. Immersion-based communication gets the brain to think *in* the new language, unlike many English as a second language (ESL) or ELD curriculums that are organized around grammatical progressions and vocabulary, which tend to emphasize thinking *about* the language. This doesn't mean that we shouldn't put up language objectives or do extra work on language. We just have to make sure that any language work that we do helps students to communicate meaningfully.

Don't overdo the use of sentence frames. In students' minds, using sentence frames can be very similar to coming up with an answer for points. Students simply say the frame first (often not knowing exactly what it means), and then they tack on a short answer at the end. Many students think that others, especially adults, are putting words into their mouths. And they're right. We must let students know that we are providing frames not to simply hear them produce "academic language" but rather to help them communicate. If the frames don't facilitate authentic communication, don't use them.

Don't focus on "correct" language use. There are many negatives that result from correcting students' language use, especially when students are talking. A great many students have worked really hard to describe their brilliant ideas in a classroom setting, only to have some minor grammar error corrected by the teacher. Too many of them get embarrassed, shut down, and stop sharing their ideas. As a result, their learning and that of the entire class suffers— sometimes for years on end.

Language is all about getting something done between people. If a message is as clear as it can be, even if it has some language that doesn't conform to common norms of correctness, then it's doing its job. Slang, incomplete sentences, gestures, non-English terms, and nonstandard uses of language can often communicate to audiences better than highly academic-sounding language. Have you ever looked at or listened to a really long sentence, summarized it in your mind, and thought, "Why didn't you just put it this way?"

Throw out your vocabulary lists. I often get a few raised eyebrows when I say this, but most lists, especially the ones that you didn't create and the ones that students have to study from, usually lead to disconnected pieces of ideas and point-motivated assessments. For most students, such lists tend to be the epitome of unmotivating. So, if you really want to have a list, *you* should use it and *you* should create it. It shouldn't come from a published curriculum, the district, or anyone else. You can make the list by analyzing reading, writing, and/or oral samples that describe the built-up idea(s) that you want students to be able to describe. For example, write a paragraph or two that describes an idea you want to see develop in your students' minds or that you want to hear from students. Then analyze the paragraph for the vocabulary that *your* students need to learn. Then teach the words as the need for them arises in context—not by having students memorize them from lists for quizzes. Memorizing word meanings and taking quizzes on them take up precious time that could be used for authentic learning.

Don't let student language development stagnate. We also need to emphasize to students that one of their responsibilities as students is to push themselves to expand their abilities to use language in a variety of ways for a variety of purposes, including ways of using it to communicate in academic and professional settings. Students need to be able to read complex texts to build up ideas in a discipline. They need to be able to use academic words and grammar to communicate in writing in different disciplines. They need to be able to speak on, listen to, and converse about increasingly complex ideas over the years. One of our big responsibilities, therefore, is to set up academic situations in which students need and want to use the most appropriate language to build up ideas and get things done. This book is meant to help you do this.

Don't miss opportunities to develop language in every activity. One of the main purposes of authentic communication and this book is to develop students' abilities to use language to communicate to, with, and from others for a wide range of purposes on a wide range of topics. When there is an engaging purpose, a need to clarify and support, and information gaps to be filled, language use and development tend to thrive. This is especially true when teachers know what language is needed and how to provide enough modeling and support for students to effectively use it to fill in the gaps, clarify terms, and support ideas needed for achieving the purpose. In the following chapters, you will see many enhancements and classroom examples that highlight ways to push for and support more robust uses of language.

SUMMARY

By now in this book you have likely begun to realize the scope and urgency of the "overhaul" that needs to happen in our schools. Students need much more engaging learning activities and purposes for fully engaging in them. They need to develop mindsets focused on building up meaningful ideas in each discipline, and they need to assume more ownership and agency over what and how they learn. We must continue to get to know our students and their needs as much as possible, and we must design instructional experiences that allow and push students to communicate. The next five chapters will help us do this.

REFLECTION QUESTIONS

1. How do your students view learning? What does learning mean to them? What mindsets about learning do they have?

2. What are the top two elements from this chapter that you would like to work on in your school or classroom? Why?

3. What are the biggest challenges you face in cultivating a culture of authentic communication in your setting?

AUTHENTIC READING

Reading is an act of civilization; it's one of the greatest acts of civilization because it takes the free raw material of the mind and builds castles of possibilities.

—Ben Okri

Think about what motivates you to read. Maybe you like good stories, so you seek out literature. Perhaps your interest in news and politics gets you to read articles, updates, or in-depth analyses of current events. As an educator you likely read to further your career and professional interests, sometimes engaging in the hard work of pushing through challenging material. Whatever the reasons, whatever the topic, your main goal is to come away with a genuine understanding of the text. This is authentic reading.

Unfortunately, a lot of reading done in school fits into the pseudo-communication category. When students see the purpose of reading as getting points, answering questions on quizzes or tests, or writing a "response" when they don't feel like responding, it's pseudo. As a result, many students lack the practice in building ideas and learning from authentic reading. For example, many students think that reading means looking at the questions first and then scanning (not reading) the associated text for language of the questions in order to quickly answer them. Their goal is often to answer the questions without reading and thinking about the text. They often learn this "skill" from taking and preparing for so many tests.

Every time students authentically read, something changes in their minds. An idea gets further clarified or is built up, decided, or born. An opinion shifts or changes completely. A new insight emerges, a new perspective takes shape, a misconception is corrected. Any text that students read should provide building blocks for ideas in some way. So how can we get this to happen? How can we improve every student's reading comprehension abilities through authentic communication activities and enhancements?

We start to answer this question by looking at what a reader's mind does when comprehending a text. This section will likely be a review for many of you, but I thought it would be helpful to show the foundational elements of the instructional enhancements that follow.

HOW READING COMPREHENSION WORKS

When a person engages in authentic reading, many thinking skills and cognitive strategies work together to understand the text. Figure 3.1 is my working model of what happens in the mind while comprehending. It is based on two decades of analyzing the research on reading, observing reading instruction, and listening to students read aloud and share their understandings. (Not coincidentally, this model looks a bit like the idea-building models you saw in Chapter 2.)

Each proficient reader uses a unique and complex mixture of comprehension strategies, thinking skills, and background knowledge to (a) strengthen and clarify one or more key ideas and (b) match what is being read to the purpose(s) for reading the text. The model in Figure 3.1 shows most of the key skills and strategies that a good reader might use to comprehend a text. The bold terms are the general skills and strategies, and the nonbold terms are examples of the skills and strategies that a person might use.

Proficient readers tend to start comprehending a text by forming a tentative initial main idea (Duke & Pearson, 2002), which is the large box on top. They use several things to get started, such as titles, images, subheadings, and the

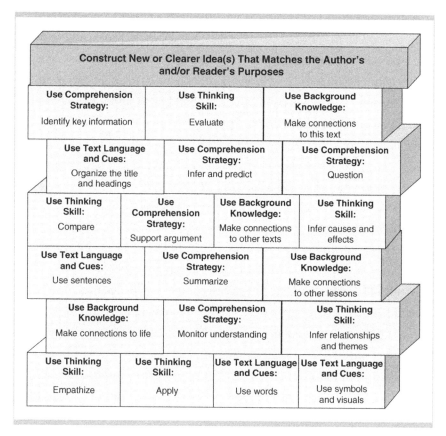

Construct New or Clearer Idea(s) That Matches the Author's and/or Reader's Purposes		
Use Comprehension Strategy: Identify key information	**Use Thinking Skill:** Evaluate	**Use Background Knowledge:** Make connections to this text
Use Text Language and Cues: Organize the title and headings	**Use Comprehension Strategy:** Infer and predict	**Use Comprehension Strategy:** Question

Use Thinking Skill: Compare	**Use Comprehension Strategy:** Support argument	**Use Background Knowledge:** Make connections to other texts	**Use Thinking Skill:** Infer causes and effects

Use Text Language and Cues: Use sentences	**Use Comprehension Strategy:** Summarize	**Use Background Knowledge:** Make connections to other lessons
Use Background Knowledge: Make connections to life	**Use Comprehension Strategy:** Monitor understanding	**Use Thinking Skill:** Infer relationships and themes

Use Thinking Skill: Empathize	**Use Thinking Skill:** Apply	**Use Text Language and Cues:** Use words	**Use Text Language and Cues:** Use symbols and visuals

Figure 3.1   Comprehension Processes Model for Reading

purpose(s) for reading the text. The reader decodes the letters of the words into sounds in order to recognize the meanings of the words (National Institute of Child Health and Human Development, 2000). Pictures in the text often help students recognize words and form initial ideas. The reader combines words into sentences and sentences into paragraphs. To decide if a sentence or paragraph makes sense enough to move on, the reader monitors his or her overall understanding. The reader also summarizes paragraphs and larger portions of text down into memorable chunks in order to reduce and organize the large amount of information. The reader also connects to different types of background knowledge, brings up and adjusts mental images, and uses other thinking skills to build up the key idea(s).

In real reading, of course, a student would not use every skill and strategy shown in the diagram. Depending on the individual and the type of text, the reader might rely heavily on just a few strategies, using them multiple times. For example, as you read this paragraph and look at the model; you are using text and visual cues (the figure); you might be asking several questions; and you refer several times to your background knowledge of how reading works, how you read, and how your students read. You might compare (thinking skill) this model to other models and lists of reading strategies. All the while, you are likely monitoring your understanding and figuring out how to apply this new information to your evolving idea about how to improve your students' reading comprehension. Purposeful building of an idea while reading means that students must learn to frequently zoom out to see if that purpose is being met—or if it needs to be modified in some way as indicated by the text's details. When students don't do this zooming in and out, comprehension tends to suffer (Harmon & Hedrick, 2000).

Throughout the reading process, good readers monitor their comprehension, which means identifying any holes in their understandings and then using appropriate strategies to solve comprehension problems (Adler, 2001). They need to make many split-second decisions about whether they have comprehended the current sentence or passage well enough to continue reading. You just did that if you are now reading this sentence. Good readers are constantly, yet mostly subconsciously, asking, "Did this part fit well enough into my main idea or purpose for this text?" If so, then they proceed. If not, they fix up their comprehension in various ways such as summarizing, rereading, looking ahead in the text, and so on.

Here is a hypothetical example of a what a student might be thinking while reading a text. The student reads a description of continental drift in a short science text. She starts by decoding the words and forming sentences. She might think, "This part shows how tectonic plates move (summarize), but I still wonder why they move (question; cause-effect thinking). I think people didn't figure this out for such a long time because we didn't have good maps that showed how the continents fit together like a puzzle (inference; using background knowledge). For evidence, they compared rocks and plants and animals on different continents (support for argument). What will the world look like millions of years from now (question)?" As she reads, she connects the text's information to related knowledge and experience in her mind that she, in a sense, uses as construction materials to reshape and build meaning as the text dictates. As she reads, she answers some of her questions (or not) and confirms her predictions and inferences (or not). She compares this evolving idea with each successive part of the text, and she modifies or discards any inconsistencies. That is, she "prunes away" the less useful information.

I included this overview of reading comprehension to provide a foundation for the enhancements that follow. It is very helpful to know all that needs to happen in the mind in order to figure out what your students need to work on during learning activities.

ENHANCING READING ACTIVITIES

This section describes authentic communication enhancements to four reading activities that are commonly used in classrooms. Even though these enhanced versions can be implemented as is, they are also meant to serve as models of the enhancement process. As you will see, there are many different ways to increase the authenticity of communication through texts. By looking at these examples and trying them out, you will hopefully see opportunities to develop your own enhancements to the many other lesson activities that you already use with your students.

Enhanced Teaching of Comprehension Strategies

There has been a lot of great work in recent decades focused on teaching students comprehension strategies (see Harvey & Goudvis, 2007; Keene & Zimmermann, 2007). Reading workshops, guided reading, and reciprocal teaching are good examples of approaches that emphasize developing comprehension strategies. In some classrooms, however, the teaching of reading strategies has gone a bit overboard, with too much focus on developing the strategies in isolation. Students need to have a solid understanding that the strategies and skills are meant to work together to construct meaningful ideas from the text.

The following suggestions detail how to enhance strategy instruction with the three features of authentic communication to help students more effectively develop their content understandings, thinking skills, language, and social skills.

Requires and Helps Students to Purposefully Build Ideas

- Set up a purposeful task or product for reading that goes beyond answering questions, writing essays, filling in boxes, or being tested on it. Think about why a person in the real world might read the text or a text similar to it. For example, students could read it in order to write a letter to a real audience, prepare a presentation, write an article, record a podcast, design a website, or choose their own way of communicating the idea(s) to others.

- Make sure that students understand that comprehension strategies (inferring, summarizing, figuring out a character's traits, connecting to background knowledge, etc.) are meant to be used to comprehend, and this comprehension is meant to help them build a larger idea. Any time a strategy comes up, either you or students should be able to describe how it helps to construct the focal idea(s).

- Use a visual organizer to record thoughts that emerge from strategy use (e.g., see the idea-building blueprint in Chapter 2 or the online appendix). Students can see their idea building on paper (in front of them or enlarged up in front of the class) as they write brief notes on their inferences, summaries, questions, etc. Model this recording of thoughts for students. Some teachers even have students use small cards or sticky notes that they can move around and stack up to show how the text is helping them build up ideas.

Requires and Helps Students to Clarify and Support

- Emphasize reading for clarity and support. This means reading at more than one level. The basic level is keeping track of and prioritizing what the text says, including identifying main ideas, plots, and details. Another level is more meta, or critical, in which students question the text and evaluate how clear or well supported it is. Students can use different symbols to indicate what is clear or unclear as well as strong support, weak support, or mediocre support.

- When orally sharing responses to a text (e.g., predictions, inferences, summaries, questions, claims) in groups or pairs, encourage listeners to ask a clarify or support question that (a) helps listeners to better understand what the talker is saying and/or (b) intentionally pushes the talker to clarify or support something that needs it. For example, if a student says, "It was about how volcanoes form," a partner should ask questions such as "How exactly? How do they know? What are examples?"

- When reading stories, tell students that in order to build up an idea (e.g., theme) as they read, they need to keep thinking about and clarifying how characters are talking, acting, and changing. They can ask themselves, "Does the character do or say unexpected things? How is the character like us? What did the author want us to learn from this character and how she or he changed?" You can model a conversation with yourself in which you say a short sentence or something in an unclear way (e.g., "I think the main character is getting nicer.") and then push yourself to be clearer and use some support (e.g., "Wait. That's not enough. I should think more about what I mean by nice and also think about the actions and words, at the beginning of the book and now, that he used to support that he is nicer...").

Requires and Helps Students to Fill Information Gaps

- Create an engaging need for students to get information from a text. Students should need to use the text's information and comprehension skills to help them build up larger conceptual understandings. Remind them that one of the purposes of reading is to get new information and insights from authors, who have a wide array of different knowledge, experiences, and perspectives to share.

- Before reading, remind students to always try to start reading any text with a goal of learning or thinking something new that will last in their brains for a long time. Model (e.g., think aloud) for students how to mentally (and physically, if desired) highlight new information that they didn't know before reading this text. ("Here's something I didn't know. This is an interesting perspective that I haven't considered before. Here, I found the information I was looking for in order to improve my idea about...")

- Assign different strategy emphases to different students in a pair or group. Students should still use other strategies, but they need to emphasize coming up with their assigned strategy. For example, Student A gets an inference card and Student B gets a question card. They read part of the text, take notes, and then meet to share their strategy thoughts and how they contribute to comprehension of the text.

Note: The next section describes the first of many classroom examples of enhancements for more and better authentic communication that you will see in this and the next four chapters of this book. In each example, there are two versions of the activity. The original version represents a typical approach to how this activity within a lesson is presented and used. The enhanced version describes the same activity in the same lesson but with key enhancements that make a difference in the quality of the communication.

CLASSROOM EXAMPLE: Enhancing Comprehension Strategy Instruction in Sixth-Grade English Language Arts

In this example from a sixth-grade classroom, the teacher was focusing on comprehension strategy instruction using the story "Eleven," by Sandra Cisneros. Both versions include mini lessons and modeling of comprehension strategies, with some student interactions, practice time, and writing. Look for ways in which the teacher added and strengthened the three features of authentic communication in the enhanced version.

Original version. The teacher planned on saying, "Okay, now I just did a mini lesson on interpreting themes from character changes by looking at their actions and words. I want you to do this as you read the story "Eleven" on your own. Then I want you to talk about your interpretations in your small groups. Finally, write down your thoughts in your journal. Remember to play your roles (e.g., facilitator, connector, note taker, harmonizer)."

Enhanced version. After the mini lesson on interpreting themes, the teacher said, "Teachers in sixth grade need your help to decide if the story "Eleven," has one or more themes that will help middle-school students become better people. Authors don't just say themes directly. They often use the words and actions of characters in the story. Your job is to look closely at how the characters talk and act and then to think about how the author might be trying to teach us something through them. Our first step we will do together. Listen carefully as I model how to do this. I will begin by reading the first page of the story, noting on the board the characters' words and actions that I find significant, and sharing my thoughts with you about how they help me to build up one or more themes, or messages, that the author is trying to teach. Try to follow my thinking so that later you can do the same. Before I let you practice on your own, I will ask you to take a moment to discuss with your partner how solid you think my evidence from the story is. Perhaps you will agree. Perhaps you will have questions or even disagree. These are all the types of thinking that good readers do when they read."

After students shared with the partners and the whole class discussed some of the points raised during partner sharing, the students were instructed to read on their own. The teacher continued, "Use sticky notes to mark interesting or important character actions and words. Once you have finished, I will give you time to arrange your sticky notes into groups of possible themes and then compare with your partners. The two of you together will build your short list of ideas and themes. As you do this, each of you will need to listen closely and ask the other questions to clarify and support your choices. For example, you could ask, 'How does that action support the theme of ...? Is this theme important to middle schoolers? Why or why not?'"

 ## Enhanced Close Reading

Close reading focuses on analyzing a portion of text to understand significant details, patterns, devices, language, or an author's craft. It can be helpful because it asks students to zoom in and consider the meanings of words, phrases, and sentences; the organization of sentences; and the text's overall development of one or more ideas. But if close reading lacks a larger purpose, or the text-dependent questions don't connect to this purpose, students can end up taking a "here's just a bunch more questions we have to answer"

approach to the work. You can use the following suggestions for enhancing close reading activities with the three features of authentic communication.

- Make sure that the text helps students to build up their big ideas and that the portion of the text to be analyzed helps students to understand the text. Avoid choosing a part that is grammatically interesting but not important for the text's meaning.

- Use questions that help students build up the big ideas in this particular text as well as questions that can be used with other texts (e.g., "Why did the author repeat certain things, insert a flashback story, not use standard grammar, use a certain symbol throughout, etc.?")

- Use the idea-building blueprint (see Chapter 2 or the online appendix) to keep track of the answers to questions and insights that come from the close reading analyses.

- In close reading discussions, remind students to push themselves to be as clear as possible so that others can benefit from their insights and answers. Remind them that, when they speak, they are helping others build ideas and become better readers—and when they listen, they are building ideas and becoming better readers.

- Model for students how to "question the author" about the clarity or support in the text. Students can write the questions on sticky notes or in margins. They can also write possible answers (e.g., "Why did the author leave this out? . . . Maybe to let me fill in the details from my experience."). Ask students to come up with suggestions for the author to better communicate to them with this text.

- When a student answers a close reading question, orally or in writing, you can pause to let listeners think of and write down any clarifying or supporting questions that they have in response to the answer. They can even quickly meet with a partner to decide which would be the best question to ask the peer who answered.

- Give different groups two different parts of the text to closely read. Have each group prepare close reading questions for the other group. You can help them. Remind students to ask questions that focus on how the passage builds up the plot, main idea(s), argument, etc. Then members from the different groups meet in pairs or small groups to share their passage and questions.

- Have students, in groups or pairs, look through a text to help you choose a passage for close reading. Remind them of the criteria for choosing: It should be grammatically or rhetorically interesting (e.g., complex sentences, figurative language, literary devices), have interesting content (e.g., controversial, unexpected, humorous), and be important for helping students build up their big idea(s). Then have students argue for their chosen passages.

- Give groups or pairs different questions to answer (like a jigsaw) about a given passage; then have them meet and share their answers.

CLASSROOM EXAMPLE: Enhancing Close Reading in Fourth-Grade History

Here are two versions of a close reading task in a fourth-grade history lesson. Notice how the second version is framed differently, involving students in a larger social debate about how we represent our common history. Also look for differences in the three features of authentic communication between the original and enhanced versions.

Original version. The essential question for the week was this: "What impact did the missions have on Native Americans in what is now California?" Students were going to create a poster presentation to answer this question. Students would closely read two articles about the missions and their effects on the people who lived in California long before the Europeans arrived. The teacher would model how to focus on a passage and take notes, asking text-dependent questions such as "Who was in charge of establishing the missions? Why did Spain establish the missions? Where does the text answer this? What terms (e.g., *herding, punish*) did the author use to cause readers to infer what Junipero Serra thought of the indigenous people? Students would answer these questions in the whole-class discussion and take notes to help them work on their posters the next day.

Enhanced version. To beef up the purpose and its engagement, the teacher changed the essential question to "Should modern cities change the names of streets and buildings from Junipero Serra to something else?" The teacher explained to students, "To help make this decision, you need to find out if Serra had a more positive or more negative impact on the people who had been living in California before the arrival of the Spanish missionaries. You will be in pairs, and half of you will read Text A and the other half, Text B. As you read, I want you to zoom in and closely read the paragraphs that are marked on each article. You and your partner need to notice and highlight the language that the author uses to present the evidence and how it supports the claim. As you read the articles, which include primary source excerpts, I also want you to stack up your reasons and evidence on each side to make an initial decision. Then A and B pairs will become a group of four to share your ideas, your focal passages, and the language that you found. Each pair should ask the other pair questions to clarify any terms they are using from the text. And most importantly, you need to decide which side's evidence and reasons weigh more."

Enhanced Text Feature Walks and Talks

Conversations about text features, such as text previews, "walks," and discussions in which the class analyzes texts can help students build up mental frameworks for constructing ideas that emerge in the text (Kelley & Clausen-Grace, 2010). Looking at features also allows students to make choices regarding what to keep in their minds as they read. There can be a lot to analyze: general features such as titles, headings, visuals, and overall organization of ideas as well as rhetorical structures such as compare-contrast, cause-effect, narration, persuasion, and so on. Analyzing these features prepares readers for using effective strategies and thinking.

To set up the text walk, a teacher usually has students look at the title along with other visual clues such as pictures, charts, subheadings, boxed text, etc. Then students think about one or more possible purposes for the text. They might use sentence stems such as the following: "To inform me of... To persuade me to... To entertain me by..." The teacher then walks through the text and facilitates a conversation about text structures and features that help students predict what will be in the text and how to approach it when they start reading it. These conversations are meant to support comprehension strategies, prompt thinking skills, and shape the inner language choices that students make in the future. What students focus on initially can influence what stays and what fades in their minds during reading, creating a framework on which to put evolving ideas, details, and ongoing summaries as they read.

- Remind students that analyzing text features before, during, and after reading is highly helpful for building up the key idea(s) in a text. During a text feature talk, model the building up of a big idea with the class's help. Partially fill in a visual such as a semantic map, Venn diagram, T-chart, or idea-building blueprint (see Chapter 2 or the online appendix), and then have students fill in the rest during reading.

- Start with an engaging essential question that the text will help to answer. Have students stop at times during the text analysis to see if and how the features might help to answer the question. This is also a chance to show students how much comprehension can come from text feature analysis—even before reading.

- Have students in small groups lead their own text feature talks. Before they start reading a text, have all students look through the text for a few minutes to prepare to lead the text feature talk. Then you choose a student from each group to lead the text talk (e.g., "Student C in each group will lead."). The leader acts like a teacher to take group members through the text. The leader or other group members should, at some point (often near the end), talk about how this text will likely help them build up their big idea(s).

Requires and Helps Students to Clarify and Support

- During text feature talks, model how to ask and answer clarifying and supporting questions. If one student poses an initial idea about the text's features, have other students prompt the talker for clarification or support. Have students keep in mind that these questions are needed to help their peers and themselves clarify and solidify important ideas that they are learning.

- Have students take notes during the text feature discussion. They can put the notes on a visual organizer, an outline, or on sticky notes. They then share notes with a partner who asks at least one or two clarification and support questions. They add to the notes based on these questions and after having partners share their ideas. Then during reading, they can edit and add, as needed. You can also have students share ideas that they got from partners during the whole class share out time.

- Give students time to individually practice analyzing features (i.e., do their own text walks). They should stop to take notes and mentally ask questions about the features (e.g., "How does this visual clarify this section? What is a parasite? Why did the author use foreshadowing here? Why is this section important?"). They can, for example, turn visuals or subheadings into questions. Then later you can look at these notes to see how well they are understanding the features of the text.

Requires and Helps Students to Fill Information Gaps

- Give A and B students different texts. By themselves, each student prepares a text feature talk on their text for the other person. A and B pair up, and the person leading prompts the partner to go through the text features and respond with predictions, insights, and questions.

- After students do their own individual text walks through the text and generate several questions about it, have them go back and answer these questions, if possible, and see how well they predicted what the text would be about. Collect their notes to get a sense of strengths and needs.

- Give students two or more texts (websites work well for this) in which you tell them they need to choose one of the texts using text feature walks. They need to look at the features to see which one will be most helpful for accomplishing the eventual performance task that helps them build and show their understanding of a big idea.

CLASSROOM EXAMPLE: Enhancing Text Feature Talks in Third-Grade Science

These two versions of a text feature analysis activity both take students through common text features and then ask them to consider how these connect to the content. Yet notice how the enhanced version creates a richer context for idea building that gives the process more meaning and purpose for using language.

Original version. The teacher planned to ask students to preread an article on interpreting data from fossils. The teacher would first read the title ("Learning From Fossils") and hold a brief class discussion after asking students what they thought, based on the title, the article was about. Then the teacher planned to walk students through the different text features of the article and have them ask questions based on pictures and subheadings (e.g., "Why is this image here? What can we learn from fossilized pollen?"). The teacher would also emphasize that this article would help them learn Next Generation Science Standards (NGSS) standard 3-LS4-1 (Analyze and interpret data from fossils to provide evidence of the organisms and the environments in which they lived long ago.), which was written up on the board. After the text walk, the teacher planned to read the article aloud, stopping at times to ask questions and clarify ideas.

Enhanced version. The teacher held up a picture of a fossil and asked pairs to share with one another their responses to this question: "What about this animal and the past might we be able to guess by studying this fossil in different ways?" The teacher also asked each pair to take notes to help them develop a possible big final idea that would serve as an answer to the question. Or they could come up with their own juicy question and buildable answer that related to the topic. Before they shared, he took a moment to model the kinds of clarifying and exploratory questions he expected partners to ask of each other ("What do you mean by...?" "What in the picture helps you interpret that?"). After the pairs had shared and taken notes, the teacher previewed the article and its features with the whole class. The teacher read the title and called on individual students to read the subheadings aloud before asking students to write down questions that they thought the article would answer. In A-B pairs, A analyzed two visuals and B analyzed two different visuals; after several minutes, they shared why they thought the author included the visuals and how these might help them answer the initial question. After reviewing these features and asking students to make inferences based on them, the teacher started to read the article with the class's help. He used a think-aloud to model his thinking about if and how the first few paragraphs were meeting expectations that they had built up with their text feature analyses. Student A in each pair read the next paragraph and stopped; then the pair discussed expectations or surprises. Then B did the same. Students read the rest of the article independently, taking notes (on a visual organizer) that helped them answer the big question using ideas from the text.

 ## Enhanced Reading of Word Problems

In math, students should read math problems not only to solve them but also in order to build up core mathematical ideas about how math works. Math teaching is often focused on developing the skills and knowledge for solving problems and getting a correct answer. Math assessments tend to rely on how many right answers students get, with less attention on the thinking that led them to the answer, and even less on the larger mathematical principles, concepts, and reasoning that students need. Yet these are the "ideas" that we want students to build. They are the ideas about how math works and the reasoning that undergirds it all. We want students to think things such as "When I divide, I am seeing how many times a number fits into another number. And if it doesn't fit perfectly, there is a remainder, which I can turn into a fraction. For example, …" or "In this type of problem we set the two equations equal to each other because that allows me to figure out both variables. One equation with two variables can't be solved, but when you have . . ."

One of the most important text types that students need to understand in school is word problems. Word problems are most often used in math and, as students get older, in science and other subjects. Word problems tend to be challenging to understand for several reasons:

- Many problems have terms and situations that are not familiar to students. They might not have had direct or indirect experiences to help them understand the situation, the context, or what is happening.

- Students might not care about the problems. They might lack the curiosity needed to motivate them enough to solve them. It's a lot of work to read and solve a word problem.

- The authors of problems often put the bare minimum of information into writing them to save space. Many authors don't try to make problems as clear as possible to a wide range of students.

- Readers need to "translate" what is happening in the written description into a mathematical situation.

- The problem scenarios and topics often jump around from one problem to the next. Students need to drastically shift their mental pictures of what is happening.

- The problems often require students to also use complex visuals such as pictures, diagrams, graphs, tables, maps, etc.

- Some authors often try to mislead or trick readers with unnecessary information or obscure terms.

To overcome these challenges, teachers use a variety of effective activities such as marking up and highlighting the text of the problem, reading the problem multiple times, creating drawings and visual organizers, and rereading problems with different focuses each time. The following enhancements can be used to make these and other math reading activities even more effective for learning.

- Remind students that they are solving these problems not for points but to build up their math skills and to build up one or more larger math ideas that can be applied to other problems (e.g., "I can use a line on a graph to extrapolate additional data not given in the problem. I can group the same number of things and add them up to see if my multiplication is okay.")

- Have students use the math version of the idea-building blueprint (see Chapter 2 or the online appendix), and include in it one or two of their own problems that they create that support the idea. They should be able to share their idea with others (e.g., "On my blueprint my idea is that you can use the ratio of distance over time to figure out the speed, and you can do speed times time to figure out the distance you travel. Here is a problem that I created to show this…."). One of their culminating tasks can be to present their blueprint to a small group of peers.

- Create interesting problems. Use the Internet or book problems to get initial problem ideas and adapt them to make them more connected to your students' lives. Change the wording a bit, use students' names, and use current events at the school.

Requires and Helps Students to Clarify and Support

- Tell students that they will read the problem twice (at least). In each reading, have them focus on different types of questions that clarify and support reasoning. For example, in the first read, have students ignore the numbers and focus on what is happening. They ask clarifying questions about what is going on, mathematically, that will lead to solution methods. In the second read, have students pose solution methods and ask each other support questions such as "What part of the problem supports that solution method? What mathematical principles or rules support that solution method?"

- Give different problems to pairs or groups. Have students collaborate to write clarifying questions for the problem, such as "What is changing? Is it a constant rate?" Even if they understand it (or think they understand it), they can put down questions they think someone else might not be clear on when they read it. Then students can meet with other pairs or groups with different problems and teach them to one another, with emphasis on clarifying and justifying solution methods.

- When students work in pairs and groups, have them push their partners to "support each statement" with lots of *why* questions. When a student poses an idea: "I think we should…" a partner should ask, "Why?" They can also ask for clarification if needed (e.g., "What does *reciprocal* mean?" "What's a root?").

- Pairs of A students and pairs of B students create problems that show the math being learned and that are engaging to fellow students. Then A and B meet, and Student B has Student A read and do the problem that B created. Student A should ask at least one clarification question that B answers. Student B helps Student A think about the problem, and once A starts solving it, A needs to describe steps and decisions. Student B asks A to justify these by using the wording of the problem and mathematical principles.

- After solving problems, have students meet with a partner to share their evolving big idea, using problems as examples. They take notes on any new ideas, principles, or problem examples that they can add to their learnings. For example, my partner might share an idea that is similar to mine but with different problems and explanations of solution methods. She says, "If you have one angle, you can usually figure out the other angles because they add up to 180 on one side or 360 for the two sides. This is always true, but the line has to be straight. One example of this is the clock problem that I made up. Every hour the short hand moves one-twelfth of the way around the clock…."

- Give pairs different information gap cards. To make the cards, extract the numbers from a word problem and put them on one card (data card). Then put the word problem's text without numbers on the other card (problem card). In pairs, the problem card partner paraphrases the problem and asks for the data to help him or her solve the problem. The data card person, before giving the data, asks the problem card partner, "Why do you need that?" The problem partner then gives justification for the data that is needed and explains what he or she will do with it to solve the problem. (See the Going Deeper section in Chapter 5 for a more detailed description.)

CLASSROOM EXAMPLE: Enhancing Reading of Word Problems in Fifth-Grade Math

The goal of this activity is to teach students how to read and understand a real-world problem and graph points on a coordinate plane in order to solve it. In both of the versions that follow, the teacher thinks aloud and models how a proficient math student might think while reading a word problem. Notice how the second version puts more focus on reading for authentic understanding.

Original version. The teacher planned to use a think-aloud in order to model three steps for reading a word problem: (1) look at the numbers and begin to draw what is happening, (2) think about one or more possible ways to solve it, and (3) then solve for the answer using appropriate units. She would walk the class through a second problem, this time engaging students by asking for their help. She planned to have students work in small groups to solve the other problems in the textbook and record their work as she had modeled earlier. Students would then trade papers with another group for feedback.

Enhanced version. The teacher began by telling students that they would work on their reading of word problems today, focusing on problems involving linear relationships and graphing them on coordinate planes. The teacher showed a picture of a small airplane and read the problem: "You are going to pilot a small plane across the United States. The last time a pilot flew the same plane across the United States, the pilot kept a log that had the distance and the time it took for the five legs of the entire trip. The log had the following entries: 1,200 miles took eight hours; 600 miles took four hours; 900 miles took six hours; 450 miles took three hours; 300 miles took two hours. You are in a hurry for this trip, so you want to fly for ten hours one day and twelve hours the next. How far will you go each day?"

She then told students to read it again and picture what was happening in their minds and draw it in some way—but without the numbers. She gave them a minute and then modeled her thinking and visualizing of the problem, drawing her visualization on the board without the numbers. Then she read it again, this time putting the numbers onto the diagram. Then she used a think-aloud in which she shared some of the clarifying questions that she had (e.g., "Does it matter that the previous pilot flew for twenty-three hours and I plan to fly for only twenty-two hours?") After sharing her thinking and having students initially think about the problem without the numbers, the teacher moved into the process of working out a solution. She asked students if they recognized any patterns in the numbers, and one student said, "You can put it into a table." She responded, "And what can we do with data tables? We can graph them…Yay! Who's excited?" She then explained how to plot points on the graph from the two columns of the table. The teacher prompted pairs to pose ideas for how to answer the problem's question using the graph. She observed them and then started a final discussion focused on how to find the new points (10 and 1,500) and (12 and 1,800) on the line in order to get the answers. Finally, she had them write down a big idea entry in their math idea journals that started with this: "With problems that have linear relationships, we can…"

SUMMARY

Students have a right to read to learn, not just read to be assessed. One of the main purposes of school should be to help students communicate as well as they can in whatever situation that arises in life. Reading is one of the most important and challenging modes of communication—not because it is so intensely tested but because there is so much power in being able to learn content and language from a wide range of texts. Large amounts of authentic reading can have a profound communication effect on students of all ages. To enhance reading activities, we often need to shore up their purposes, make sure reading helps students to build up ideas, and craft situations in which the text provides needed information.

REFLECTION QUESTIONS

1. How might you learn more about how much and how well your students are reading authentically versus reading in pseudo-communication ways?

2. Think of a common reading activity (e.g., reading logs, reader's theater, genre analysis, graphic organizers, story retelling, silent reading, analyzing texts for themes) that you use with your students. How authentic is it? How strong are the three features of authentic communication? How might it be enhanced?

3. How authentic are your reading assessments?

AUTHENTIC LISTENING

Imagine the world we could build if everyone truly listened.

Given that we do so much listening in life, it behooves us to be good at it. And yet, many adults are not good listeners. One reason is that a great many of us didn't work on improving our listening very much when we were in school. Another reason is that we tend to value what *we* think and say over what others are thinking and saying. Still another reason is that good listening is a lot of mental work, and unless we see the value of it, we tend to only listen well for a few minutes at most. Fortunately, there are things that we can do for our students in school to help them become better listeners now, in future classes, and for when they become adults.

Many students still need to work on listening to directions, stories, and rules, but the focus of this chapter is on helping students improve at building up robust ideas by listening to longer and more academic spoken messages. These include lectures, TED Talks, podcasts, speeches, news programs, nonfiction read-alouds, presentations, explanations, arguments, documentaries, think-pair-shares, etc.

Schools tend to spend very little time or energy on intentionally teaching and improving listening skills, particularly after students leave third grade. Why? First, it isn't tested much and it's very hard to see inside a brain that is listening. Second, teachers tend to assume that students have learned to listen to a wide range of oral messages in previous classrooms or at home. Third, even though new standards include more listening skills, it doesn't mean that we know how to teach or assess them very well. So we have some major work to do.

HOW LISTENING COMPREHENSION WORKS

The main goal of listening, as shown in the top box of the diagram in Figure 4.1, is constructing one or more ideas that match the purpose(s) of the speaker and/or listener. In the top box is the idea(s) that is being built up, changed, or clarified inside a student's mind. It's a bit messy because the brain uses the four dimensions (background knowledge, language skills, thinking skills, comprehension strategies) that contribute to understanding, as you can see.

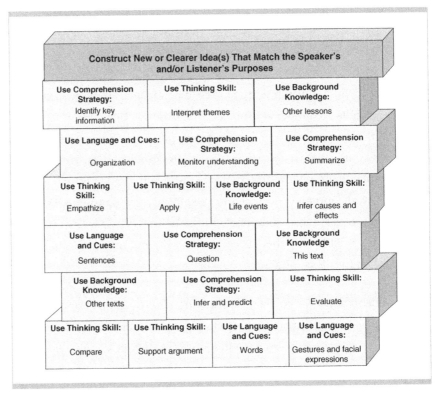

Figure 4.1 Comprehension Processes Model for Listening

You saw a very similar diagram in the Chapter 3 (see Figure 3.1). This is because reading and listening comprehension are similar in many ways. For example, readers and listeners tend to use strategies such as summarizing, questioning, and inferring along with thinking skills such as comparing, interpreting, empathizing, and so forth. Readers and listeners also do a lot of connecting and comparing to existing background knowledge. If you have ever both read a book and listened to an audio version of it, you likely have noticed the similarities and differences.

Authentic listening means comprehending meaningful oral messages in order to build up one or more ideas. The listener builds up the idea by monitoring his or her understanding, clarifying and supporting the idea with details and evidence, some of it coming from the message and some from the listener's background knowledge. A good listener focuses on the meaning of the sentences and paragraphs, pays attention to nonverbal and prosodic cues, and frequently summarizes sections into chunks. From beginning to end, a good listener monitors overall understanding based on the purpose for listening. (Refer to Chapter 3 for more details on what the mind does to comprehend.)

Now, for fun, create a similar diagram that shows a specific instance of listening by your students or by you. Put the idea or purpose on top, and then write down possible skills and strategies that your students (or you) use to comprehend.

AUTHENTIC LISTENING ACTIVITIES

You are already using many activities and routines with lots of listening in them, and you are already making enhancements to meet the needs of your students. My hope is that you will learn some additional enhancements here and that you will see the urgency and power of working on the three features of authentic communication in every activity.

Enhanced Think-Pair-Shares (With an Emphasis on Listening)

Think-pair-shares (aka turn-and-talks, pair-shares) are used by many teachers these days. This is mostly a good thing because students are getting some practice in talking and listening to other human beings. Pair-shares are often quick exchanges of answers between two students. Yet many pair-shares could and should be more academically and socially productive in several key ways. First of all, most pair-shares highlight the talking, often lacking a consistent and clearly stated focus on high-quality listening. Here are some suggestions for improving listening in pair-shares in authentic ways. (Note: In Chapter 5 you will see an example of a pair-share that is enhanced with an emphasis on strengthening speaking.)

Requires and Helps Students to Purposefully Build Ideas

- Make sure the think-pair-share has a purpose beyond just practicing oral output and listening. Students should be helping each other build up one or more ideas to accomplish a meaningful task or project. The student should be able to answer, "Why am I listening to my partner?" If there is no good reason, the listening will not likely be authentic—nor will the talking, for that matter.

- Make sure that students understand how to apply listening comprehension strategies (inferring, summarizing, asking questions, etc.) and thinking skills in service of building up an idea in the discipline. Use the idea-building blueprint (see Chapter 2 or the online appendix) or some other organizer to show the elements and "materials" used to build up ideas while listening to partners. Have students use the organizer to remind themselves and those speaking to them to focus on helping them build up the idea in the organizer.

Requires and Helps Students to Clarify and Support

- Provide some time before listening for students to prepare to build up the idea that the speaker will be talking about. Have students think about what aspects and evidence they already have and what they think they still need. Encourage them to think things such as "What do I still need to clarify and how might listening to Alex help?" "I hope I get some more good evidence from listening to the Sofia's presentation." "What new idea about gravity can I start building up today by listening to my partner?" "How will what I listen to in the pair-share help me to prepare for my project or presentation?"

- Model for students (e.g., have a student model with you up front) how to zoom in on certain key unformed ideas, terms, evidence, or explanations that they think could be clearer. Push them to ask others (peers, friends, teachers, family members, etc.) questions that (a) help them (the listeners) understand something better and build up an idea of what the speaker is saying and/or (b) intentionally push the speakers to clarify or support something that needs it (i.e., to help the talkers communicate their ideas to others).

- Require students to ask clarify and/or support questions as they are listening to partners share. Some teachers even have them put a chip or card down in front of them to show that they have asked a question. Remind students that, even though at times they might not think their partners need to clarify or support, prompting them to do so often brings up new information and also helps the speaker organize and remember what they are saying. Also remind listeners that the questions should help them to build up ideas, not just to put cards down or to make you happy.

- For longer oral messages by the talker, provide some guidance for what to listen for. For example, if talkers are sharing an argument that they will eventually write down, have listeners listen closely for the main claim, the clarity and strength of the evidence or reasoning used to support it, any loaded language, and how honestly the person presents the counterclaim, if at all. For older students, I would also have them try to listen for the main criteria used by the partner to judge and compare evidence on both sides of the argument. Students can also take notes on graphic organizers.

Requires and Helps Students to Fill Information Gaps

- Create an engaging *need* to listen to the speaker. When students know that they will benefit in some way from listening to their partners, they listen better and ask more authentic questions. For example, when students need what they learn from pair-share partners to give a presentation, analyze data, or complete a project, they need to listen to build up the idea that they will communicate.

- Remind students to always try to start listening with a purpose of learning or thinking something new. Using a think-aloud, model for students how to mentally (and physically through annotation, if desired) highlight new information that they didn't know before as they listen to a partner's message.

- Make sure that speakers have enough content to have something useful and meaningful to say. If you think both students in a pair-share will have the same answer, you can (a) ask two different questions, one for each student, or (b) give A and B different topics or texts.

CLASSROOM EXAMPLE: Enhancing Think-Pair-Shares in Fourth-Grade English Language Arts

Both versions of this activity focus on think-pair-share activities to launch students' learning from the novel *Shiloh* (Naylor, 1991), which is about a boy trying to protect an abused dog. Both versions focus on a pivotal moment in the first chapter, and they both ask students to share their thoughts with each other and then report back to the class. Look for the authentic communication differences between the two.

Original version. After reading part of the first chapter aloud and asking several questions about the text to check for comprehension, the teacher planned to ask students to turn and talk to one another and answer this question: "What do you think it means when the narrator observes 'And then I feel my heart squeeze up the way he [Shiloh, the dog] stops smiling'"? Students would turn and talk and share their answers. After a minute or two, the teacher planned to ask students to share their answers with the class.

Enhanced version. After reading part of the first chapter aloud and asking several questions about the text to check for comprehension, the teacher had all students look at the line in the text, "I get to the front stoop and say, 'Go home, boy.' And then I feel my heart squeeze up the way he stops smiling, sticks his tail between his legs again, and slinks off." The teacher wrote the first of two questions on the board for the first half of the think-pair-share: "Why do you think the boy goes from saying to the dog, 'Go home, boy' to then saying his heart is squeezing up? What does that mean?"

The teacher continued, "Partner B will start. But first, can someone who is a Partner A tell the class what you do as you listen and after listening to your partner?" One student responded, "We ask at least one clarify or support question." The teacher said, "Great. Remember to listen carefully because their response might help you to build up your comprehension of the book and come up with important themes that the author is trying to teach us. And when B is finished, Partner A can also share any additional insights, ideas, or clarifications—you can paraphrase, but don't just repeat what B said; try to say something new that extends your or their understanding. Okay, now take thirty seconds to think about how you might answer this question. Thirty seconds. Go." The teacher circulated to listen in and help students with their questions (e.g., "Nice job asking for clarification when your partner said 'felt bad.'") After a couple minutes the teacher said, "Okay, now we will have several students share out ideas that they heard from their partners or, even better, a synthesis or combination of both your ideas. As we all listen, take more notes for any potential building blocks on your idea-building blueprint. And as some of you share out, I want to hear others ask clarify and support questions." The teacher did this process again with a second question: "Why is what we just focused on potentially important for the rest of the book?" Partner A started this time.

Enhanced Read-Alouds

In a read-aloud, the teacher reads a text out loud, stopping at times to help students think about or understand challenging parts of the text. The text is usually a bit more challenging than what students can read on their own. In some cases, students read along with their own texts, but this section focuses on read-alouds in which listeners don't have the text in front of them.

When listening to stories, many students tend to just listen for what happens next. Thus, one challenge is to develop students' awareness, while listening, of key literary features such as settings; character traits; problems; obstacles; resolutions; inner changes in characters; themes; and techniques such as foreshadowing, figurative language, and irony. As you come up with enhancements, think about how authors and storytellers use these things to communicate to listeners. They didn't put these things into stories so that someone could turn them into test questions.

We also need to better prepare students for listening to informational texts. As in reading, it requires different types of thinking and organization of thoughts in the brain. Informational texts tend to organize their ideas in several different ways: sequence, cause-effect, claims with support, description (often with headings and examples), problem-solution, and comparison.

Many students struggle to comprehend when listening to informational texts for several reasons:

- They haven't been immersed over time in reading or listening to informational texts. They haven't needed to work on their listening comprehension abilities, especially for longer nonfiction messages.

- They don't know what information to zoom in on and hold on to because they are not sure what the purpose of listening is. If the purpose is to be tested, then they often get overwhelmed, thinking that they need to know everything they hear.

- They miss prosodic and visual cues that indicate importance or different hierarchies of information (e.g., claim and evidence for the claim).

So how do we make it so students both want to and are able to effectively listen to a variety of complex texts that are read aloud to them? Here are some suggestions.

Requires and Helps Students to Purposefully Build Ideas

- Make sure that the skills and language that you focus on (whenever you stop and discuss the text) help students to build up at least one engaging idea. This idea might start with the text, or it might be one that students started building up in previous lessons.

- Have students take notes on a visual organizer like a semantic map or the idea-building blueprint (see Chapter 2 or the online appendix), and have students use it to remind them to focus on building an idea as they listen and as they engage in other activities that connect to what they are listening to.

- Have a final performance-related purpose for the listening such as a project, speech, letter, painting, poster, presentation, drama, website, podcast, etc.

Requires and Helps Students to Clarify and Support

- Preview the text, and put notes in it to remind you where to stop to clarify content or language, where to model how to listen and take notes on the important parts, and where to use any other needed listening comprehension strategies (e.g., summarize, infer, question).

- Give some guidance for what to listen for. For example, if it's an argument, have students listen closely for the main claim and the evidence or reasoning used to support it. If it's a story, have them listen for character development, inner and outer conflicts, major events, dialogue, symbols, themes, etc.

- When reading aloud, stop at times to have students ask each other in pairs (or ask you, if you are in whole-class mode) a clarify or support question that helps them understand something better and build up an idea of what the text is about.

Requires and Helps Students to Fill Information Gaps

- Choose a read-aloud text that students haven't read before and contains unfamiliar characters, places, plots, concepts, etc.

- Create an engaging need to listen. Ask a thought-provoking question, or show a mysterious image beforehand. Emphasize that listening right now might be the only way to get the information that they will need or want.

- Give different groups of students "secret listening" tasks in which, let's say, half of the students listen for causes and effects and the other half listens for bias. Afterward they share their notes in pairs with the other group. You can give them cards with these tasks on them.

- Listen to an audio recording of a text and model, thinking aloud and taking notes up front on how to mentally highlight new information that you didn't know before listening to this.

- If it's a picture book, cut the pages out of the book (cut up two books if there is text on the opposite sides of pictures), put the corresponding text on the back of the picture pages and laminate them, read them aloud, and post them so all can see the story progression. Do follow-up activities using the pictures.

CLASSROOM EXAMPLE: Enhancing a Teacher Read-Aloud in Third-Grade English Language Arts

This classroom example shows the different enhancements that a teacher made to a read-aloud activity partway through their reading of the novel *Because of Winn-Dixie* by Kate DiCamillo (2000). Students had been working on interpreting themes in short stories and novels. Most students had started building up variations of a theme about how making friends can help a person cope with loss. Notice how the enhanced version strengthens the three features of authentic communication, with a focus on listening.

Original version. After asking for volunteers to recap the selection from *Because of Winn-Dixie* that the class had read previously, the teacher planned to start reading aloud where they had left off, stopping at times to ask the class reading strategy-based questions that focused on key parts of the story (e.g., "What do you predict will happen next? Why? Why do you infer that she did that? What has happened so far?"). She planned to have students take notes so that they could better remember the story and to help them write a response to literature essay using the rubric they would use for the district writing assessment in two months.

Enhanced version. The teacher prepared for the day's read-aloud by putting sticky notes in places to stop and prompt students to ask clarification questions and to think about possible problems and themes. Before reading aloud, she again reminded students (a) to enjoy becoming immersed in a good story and playing the movie of it in their minds; (b) to listen for and think about the main problem or challenge to overcome, including any challenges that might be in the main character's mind; and (c) that their listening will help them to build up ideas about the story that they will use in their final project (an article for the local newspaper describing how the story helps readers understand how to face life's challenges). Each time she stopped to discuss what was on the sticky notes, she had students answer in pair-shares first before having some students share with the whole class. As students engaged in whole-class share-outs, at times she held up a pink or blue card to prompt students to ask a clarifying or supporting question of the person who shared. Depending on what was shared, the teacher took extra time to ask the class if they wanted to add any clarifications or evidence to the two whole-class idea-building blueprints for two themes from the novel that they had been developing (e.g., "Making new friendships can help us heal after losing something or someone." "Inner courage is important in life." One student even said, "We need to be like dogs and like everybody.") After the teacher finished reading the passage, she had students turn and tell each other any new information gained that might help them to write their final article.

 ## Enhanced Listening to Presentations

Even though there still tends to be too much teacher talk in lessons around the world on any given day, there will always be a need for the teacher to present ideas to the class and for students to listen effectively. You can do four general things to help students learn more and better through listening: (1) enhance your presentations (including lectures) with authentic communication features; (2) have students practice listening to longer, more complex oral presentations; (3) help students improve their presentations to other students; and (4) help students improve their note-taking skills.

Presentations, lectures, and speeches require different types of listening, depending on the genre. Narrations require listeners to listen for characters, problems, themes, etc. (see the Enhanced Read-Alouds section in this chapter); explanations require listeners to break things down and see how they fit together; problems require listeners to see the problem's components and figure out the best ways to solve it; and arguments require listeners to identify the positions or sides that are being argued, infer speaker bias, and evaluate the strength of evidence used. The better students are at recognizing the genre and listening for the key parts of it, the better their comprehension.

One of the problems with typical lecturing and note-taking for taking tests is that students tend to feel like the main purpose of notetaking is to write down everything that may be on a test. They often lack a sense of agency because they struggle to determine what is important, what to highlight, and what to leave out. They often think that they will be tested on everything. They tend to worry more about memorizing a wide range of pieces than about building up larger ideas. As you look at the recommendations that follow, consider how you might use them to foster student agency, engagement, and confidence in their abilities to learn and build complex ideas while listening to presentations.

Requires and Helps Students to Purposefully Build Ideas

- Come up with a juicy question, enigmatic image, or attention-getting anecdote that gives students some motivation and focus for the idea that they are supposed to build while listening (e.g., "How did humans influence the evolution of the peppered moth?" "What are gravity waves?" "What do ants and bees and humans have in common?")

- Don't focus on tests. Think about ways to create a more interesting task or product for which students need to listen to the information. Have students use an idea-building blueprint (see Chapter 2 or the online appendix) or other visual organizer for taking notes that help them build up an idea.

- Shorten the presentation if it's longer than ten minutes. Half of the students' age is a decent time goal (e.g., five minutes for ten-year-olds) for what they can listen to before they need to do something with the information.

Requires and Helps Students to Clarify and Support

- As they listen, have each student write down a certain number of clarify or support questions in their notes, and tell them that you will randomly call on them to ask a question during or after the presentation.

- Pause the presentation at times to have students, in pairs, answer key questions that you pose. They can quickly write down an answer and then share it with a partner. They should not read it out loud, and they should try to make it as clear as possible for the partner. Have partners who are listening ask the partner who is sharing to clarify or support if they give responses that are too short or unclear (e.g., "Tell me more about…" "What did the teacher say to support that idea?").

- Use plenty of visuals, gestures (have students do these gestures too), and repetition to make complex ideas clear and memorable. Give them cues, and pause to give them time to take notes or fill in part of an organizer.

- During or after the presentation or lecture, have students (individually or in pairs) write a one-sentence or one-paragraph synthesis using several key terms from the presentation (e.g., Manifest Destiny, expansion, virtues, rights, peace). Have students meet with other individuals or pairs to share their syntheses in order to add to or clarify them.

Requires and Helps Students to Fill Information Gaps

- In certain presentations, tell students that (a) they are about to listen to information that will help them build up idea(s) needed for doing well on their final products, and (b) this will be the only time that they will get this information.

- To prepare for a teacher presentation, observe students and talk to them in order to know what information they need the most for building up their target ideas and accomplishing any final projects or tasks that reinforce and show their learning.

- For student presentations, make sure that (a) students have different topics so listeners are not listening to information that they have heard or focused on already, and (b) there is a need to listen and to obtain the information from presenters. This might include presentations partway through a project (not at the end) in which students need the information shared by peers to incorporate into and improve their own projects. Have students fill in a visual organizer such as a semantic map or idea-building blueprint (see Chapter 2 or the online appendix).

CLASSROOM EXAMPLE: Enhancing a Teacher Presentation in Eighth-Grade History

In both versions of the presentation, the teacher presents key facts and thinking about President Andrew Jackson's influence on American history and politics. While both versions focus on unfamiliar and complex terms, consider how the enhanced version sets a context and purpose for meaningful engagement that goes beyond just assessing students' knowledge.

Original version. The teacher planned to give a presentation on Andrew Jackson's influence on American history and politics. She planned to start the presentation by telling students that they would need to listen because the information that she would share is not in the text, but it would be on the test. She would ask students to take notes in their history notebooks. When any new terms came up on the slides, she would define them and have students engage in pair-shares to explain what the terms mean. At the end of the presentation she planned to have students write a summary that they would hand in before the end of class.

Enhanced version. The teacher started the presentation by putting up a twenty-dollar bill and said, "The government is thinking that Andrew Jackson might not have been a worthy enough president to be on our currency. They need our help to decide if his overall contributions to our country and history were more positive or negative. We need to build up both sides and then determine which side's evidence and reasoning are heavier." The teacher continued to explain slides with major points from Jackson's presidency. When new terms came up, she used images with actions and words to explain them. She paused twice to say, "Okay, write down a clarification question for me.... Now share it with a partner.... Now three students please share different ones with the whole class." Students had colored cards of different sizes on which they were taking notes: green for positive evidence and orange for negative. The stronger the evidence, the bigger the card. The teacher paused at times to allow them to write and to have them meet in pairs to compare cards, especially to explain why certain cards were bigger than others. The teacher reminded them that people have different values that cause them to evaluate differently. She also reminded students that all sources, including her, can be biased and that students should always have a voice inside their heads that asks, "Where did this person get this information? How biased is it?" After the presentation, students read several short texts about Jackson and his influence in order to edit and fill in more evidence cards for each side. Finally, they put the cards onto an argument balance scale (described in Chapter 6) to evaluate the overall weight of the evidence supporting each side and decided which is heavier. They worked in pairs to write letters to the government, with the balance scale as a helpful organizer, explaining their decision.

The following set of enhancements focuses on whole-group instruction in math, which usually is in the form of teacher lectures, mini lectures, modeling, and explanations. The main question to answer here is "How can I help my students listen better and longer so that they can effectively solve this unit's problems and, more importantly, build up the concept or idea that the problems are meant to show and teach?" The key ideas that we want to build are related to how math works, how and why to solve problems in certain ways, and the reasoning that undergirds these. We want students to show and support ideas about math by using problems as concrete examples.

One of our big challenges in math is that students have the deeply ingrained habit of focusing their listening on the easiest way to solve a problem. They tend to listen to the math teacher to quickly solve problems on their homework, a quiz, or a test. They don't tend to listen to the reasoning shared by the teacher, nor do they do much reasoning while they are listening (often because they aren't given time or prompting to do much reasoning). Of course, if the teacher or talker is not describing any reasoning, the listener can't listen to it. But, ideally, a good math listener will always be listening to build up math concepts, which increases authenticity.

Requires and Helps Students to Purposefully Build Ideas

- Have dedicated times when students work on their listening to different aspects of math such as listening to: a long word problem and comprehending what is happening; multiple ways of solving a problem; mathematical reasoning; or a big math idea in which the speaker uses problems to show examples of it. Depending on the focus, have students take notes, fill in visuals, or think about how to create their own problems to show and support the big idea.

- Presenters (you or students) should share as much reasoning as possible while solving and thinking about problems. Mathematical reasoning tends to consist of (a) justifying procedures for solving problems by using mathematical principles and the description of the problem and (b) making claims, conjectures, and generalizations based on observing mathematical patterns and surprises.

- Use the math idea-building blueprint (see Chapter 2 or the online appendix), or some version of it, for taking notes on how the problems are examples that show key components supporting the idea. Remind students that they are doing problems not for points but rather to learn how math works.

Requires and Helps Students to Clarify and Support

- When presenting, stop the presentation at times to push for clarify and support questions about mathematical ideas (e.g., "I am pausing right now expecting at least one clarify and one justify question." For example, you might ask the meaning of a term that you are using or why you are doing a certain procedure. You can also stop to have students clarify and justify (support) ideas in pairs. For example, "Partner A, tell Partner B what mathematical idea these three problems are trying to teach us."

- Have students write down a certain number of clarify or support questions in their notes; they must ask one orally (in pairs or to the presenter) during the presentation. Have students signal you in some way if a peer asks a question they also have in their notes. If you get a lot of signals for certain questions, spend more time answering them.

- Based on students' struggles and confusions that you have noticed in their reasoning or problem-solving procedures, tell students what to listen for (e.g., "I have noticed that many of you have been forgetting to balance equations this week. So in this presentation, I want you to listen super closely to times when the presenter balances, attempts to balance, or forgets to balance the equation in the problem. When you do, give me this signal.").

Requires and Helps Students to Fill Information Gaps

- Remind students that listening well helps them learn new ways to solve problems and build up new mathematical ideas that will serve them throughout life.

- Have students create their own problems that support the key ideas they are building—to act as teachers, in a sense. They can create the problems individually or in pairs, and then they read them aloud to others who need to listen well in order to solve them.

- Tell students that they will need to share their evolving big ideas with several peers at the end of the week in some way and that they need to use problems that they listened to, solved on their own, solved in groups, and created on their own in order to bulk up their ideas.

Both versions of this presentation focused on introducing students to the concept of ratios and how they are used. An important feature distinguishing the enhanced version from the original is providing a more engaging purpose for listening. Notice this and how the other authentic communication features are developed when you compare the two versions.

Original version. The teacher planned to put the standard for using ratios on the board and define the term *ratio*. Then she would ask students to turn to a partner and use the term *ratio* in a sentence. Then she would use a document camera to model how to solve word problems on ratios. At times she would stop and ask students what to do to solve the problem and why. She knew that several of the same students would likely raise their hands each time that they were asked for responses. She expected that these students would help to move the presentation along. She would end by asking if anyone has any questions and would tell students which problems to solve until the class period ends.

Enhanced version. The teacher told the class, "You will teach an important idea about ratios to four other students in the class at the end of the week. You will build up this idea on the math idea-building blueprint (see Figure 4.2) to help you keep track of sample problems and how they support your idea. Listen to my presentation, take notes, and use one of the problems that I show for your blueprint. As you listen, I also want you to write down clarification questions and *why* questions about how ratios work. I will pause at times to have you share these questions and answers with a partner. The teacher started off by showing a picture of a space capsule descending with its parachutes. She asks, "The capsule just opened its chutes. What information might NASA want to know, mathematically speaking, about this capsule right now?" Students eventually come up with starting altitude and speed of descent, which would allow NASA to determine the time it will take to reach the ground. She said that even if they didn't know the altitude, they knew the average descent was 10 miles for every 30 minutes.

She then modeled how to come up with a table and a formula to help the NASA folks. The teacher used several other speed and cost problems to show how to fill in rate tables and solve problems. She paused at times to ask two types of reasoning questions: "Why did we do that procedure?" and "What kinds of math rules or patterns do you notice?" After the presentation she had students work together to solve similar problems. She reminded them that a main purpose of doing problems is to build up big ideas for how the math works—not just to make her happy or to get points. Finally, pairs created their own problems similar to the those shown by teacher and in the book, only more interesting. Students then traded problems and solved them. The teacher reminded students that they should include at least one problem that they created and at least one that their peers created on the blueprint to show in their final presentations.

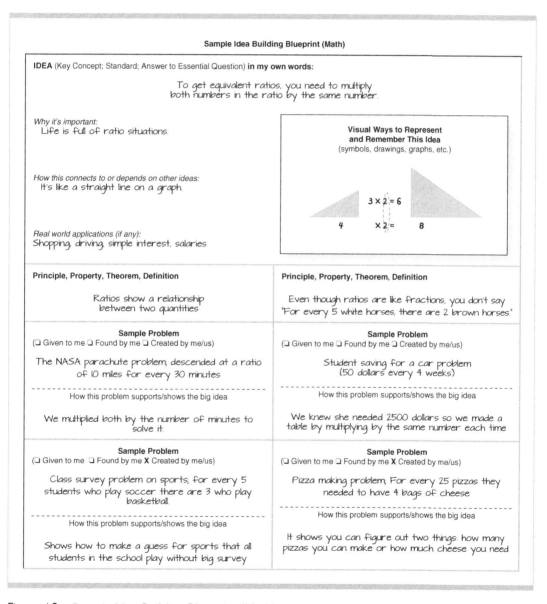

Figure 4.2   Sample Idea-Building Blueprint (Math)

SUMMARY

School provides a fertile ground for growing students' abilities to listen to a variety of messages for a variety of academic purposes. Yet a lot of listening in school has been pseudo-communication, which hasn't pushed students to practice and hone their listening skills each year. This chapter described and modeled enhancements that are meant to establish purposes, help students clarify and support ideas, and fill information gaps in order to improve the quantity and quality of student listening. I zoomed in on four commonly used listening activities, but I am hoping, as in other chapters, that you will also look at how to make these types of enhancements to other listening activities that you use. Listening is a vital skill for all arenas in life, and the better students get at it, the more enriched their lives will be—and the better off the world will be.

REFLECTION QUESTIONS

1. What are your students' strengths and weaknesses when it comes to listening?

2. Which enhancements in this chapter seem to be most useful in your setting?

3. Think of a common activity that either intentionally develops listening or depends a lot on listening. How authentic is it? How strong are the three features of authentic communication? How might it be enhanced?

AUTHENTIC SPEAKING

*Students must have plenty of opportunities to use language—
not just practice using it.*

One of the most important educational frontiers is improving classroom talk, which I have divided into two chapters, this one and Chapter 7. Chapter 7 focuses on back-and-forth conversation between students. This chapter focuses on more one-way talk, such as the talk used to answer teacher questions; give oral presentations; and share ideas with others in think-pair-shares, gallery walks, and jigsaws.

The type of speaking developed in this chapter is "multisentence"—that is, the speaking should help listeners build up important ideas in their minds, which usually requires the speaker to use two or more connected sentences. Ideally, students improve at organizing these sentences into paragraphs and using effective prosodic and nonverbal cues. For example, if I am asked to share with a partner my description of how islands form, I share several sentences with clarifications and examples. I also use hand gestures, emphasize certain words with my voice, and make a simple drawing in order to help her visualize and construct the idea in her mind as she listens to me.

When sharing an idea orally, there is no set "right" way to describe the idea. It varies depending on the speaker and the listeners. In fact, our ability to put our ideas into the right words for all those who listen is always developing as we mature and grow. (And it's one of the most important skills students need for life* too.) For these reasons, our students need lots of practice speaking to a wide variety of people about a wide range of topics. But, as any classroom teacher knows, it can be difficult to get all students to talk about what they are learning.

One of the challenges of speaking is how public it is. While writing is often seen only by the teacher, talking is heard by others—often by the whole class. Talk is highly connected to identity, self-esteem, and self-image. It's risky to share academic ideas for fear of being wrong, of making a grammar or vocabulary mistake, or of being labeled overly studious. This challenge is intensified by the fact that many students, especially after Grade 3, do not see much value in speaking to other students in class about academic topics. If they do talk about what they are learning, it is often the bare minimum. They might talk up a storm at lunchtime about nonacademic things, but then in class they talk very sparingly about the things we want them to talk about.

Talk is essential for learning for several reasons. First, it pushes students to put evolving and sometimes unclear ideas into words for others. The "for others" is important. If the others are not really listening, or if a speaker is just speaking so that the teacher hears it to give participation points, not as much learning will stick in the student's brain. There is extra thought-energy when a real person is really listening. Second, talking can help the listeners learn. Students are often very good at explaining ideas to their peers (sometimes better than adults). Third, speaking provides opportunities for language development: Students push themselves to use and try out new language for listeners, and listeners get to hear different ways of expressing academic ideas. These things will happen more often and effectively when the speaking is authentic.

So how do we encourage students to talk authentically? How do we make it safe, engaging, and useful? First, as described in Chapter 2, we need to work hard to create and maintain a classroom culture that is safe, one where students feel they can take risks and where their comments will be welcomed, useful, and appreciated. Beyond this, we must create opportunities for them to "tinker with" and "try out" the draft versions of their ideas with listeners in order to benefit from their feedback, comments, perspectives, and extra knowledge that listeners might provide.

For example, Alan reads a story about friendship and sacrifice and begins to form an idea about how good friends sacrifice time for one another. He shares his idea with a partner who asks him several clarifying questions, such as "What does sacrifice mean to you? How does it build up friendship? What are examples? Is that the most important aspect of friendship?" He answers these but continues to ponder them after answering these questions in class. By the time school has ended for the day, he has a stronger idea. The next day he tells his teacher about a time when he sacrificed going to movies to help a friend do some homework. That evening he watches a movie in which the main character makes sacrifices for a friend. He tells his group in class the next day about the movie. Speaking to others helps this idea to keep building up—and, like many important ideas, it will keep building up and changing throughout life.

Figure 5.1 shows a model that can be used to help students express ideas to others through speaking. You start with the purpose in the WHY box. Students can ask and answer the questions and even answer additional questions such as "Will what I share help a classmate improve a project that she is working on? Will a podcast persuade the city to fix the swings at the park? Will my presentation inform people about the harmful effects of using drugs? Why is this presentation worth my time and energy?"

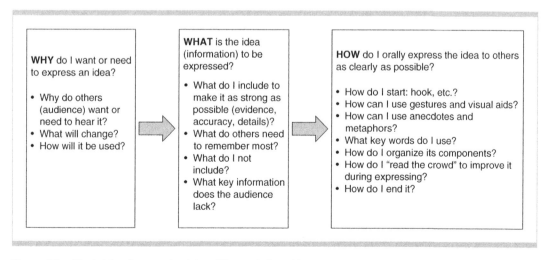

WHY do I want or need to express an idea?

- Why do others (audience) want or need to hear it?
- What will change?
- How will it be used?

WHAT is the idea (information) to be expressed?

- What do I include to make it as strong as possible (evidence, accuracy, details)?
- What do others need to remember most?
- What do I not include?
- What key information does the audience lack?

HOW do I orally express the idea to others as clearly as possible?

- How do I start: hook, etc.?
- How can I use gestures and visual aids?
- How can I use anecdotes and metaphors?
- What key words do I use?
- How do I organize its components?
- How do I "read the crowd" to improve it during expressing?
- How do I end it?

Figure 5.1   Model for Expressing Ideas Through Speaking

Second, students build or cobuild an idea (the WHAT) that will work for the purpose in the first box. They focus on making the idea as strong as possible, meaning that they choose the best evidence, examples, and reasoning to support it and bulk it up. They also think about what others will need to know and remember the most, and they try to make it as accurate as possible. They also consider what *isn't* important enough to include, knowing that listeners have a limited capacity to remember what they listen to, and they don't want to distract listeners with lots of information that may not be significant or even relevant.

Third, speakers think about HOW to most clearly express the idea. As you can see in the box, there are many considerations, all of which depend on what the audience needs. What will make it as clear as possible for a certain person or group of people? This means that the audience shouldn't always be the teacher. We want students to be able to express ideas to a wide range of people, young and old. And to do this, students should think about the best beginnings and endings, body language, visuals, anecdotes, language, organization, and so on. Much more than we tend to realize, a lot of speaking that students do in class is not authentic. Students speak to please the teacher, to get a good grade on a speech, to look like they are talking in a pair-share, or to obligatorily give an answer when called on in a class discussion. So, in order to increase the quantity and quality of authenticity in speaking-heavy activities in school, here are some enhancement suggestions.

AUTHENTIC SPEAKING ACTIVITIES

Here are four common speaking activities with authentic communication enhancements. As in other chapters, I can include only a handful of classroom samples from different grade levels and content areas. These are meant to be more detailed examples for you to analyze and, using your creativity (see Chapter 8), apply ideas from them to other activities and practices that you already do. Of course, I also hope you will find some new strategies that you will try out and get excited about using over time.

 ### Enhanced Think-Pair-Shares (With an Emphasis on Speaking)

As promised, the enhancement emphasis for think-pair-shares in this chapter is on increasing the quantity and quality of authentic speaking. In the average run-of-the-mill think-pair-share (aka turn-and-talk), the teacher asks students to pair up and tell their partners something. Often the authenticity is hit or miss, depending on the engagement of the students and the prompt.

The following enhancements are especially important for students who need more practice putting their ideas into words—many of whom tend to use avoidance strategies that teachers often don't notice, such as not speaking first and hoping time runs out while the partner is speaking, just asking questions, saying "you took my idea," "I agree," or something along these lines. What we want to do is support students to push themselves and their partners to get a lot more out of sharing ideas with each other.

Requires and Helps Students to Purposefully Build Ideas

- Make sure that students have a purpose to share that goes beyond just the think-pair-share time. Remind students that by sharing an idea that is as clear and strong as possible, they are better preparing themselves and partners to accomplish an upcoming task or project. And they are getting vital practice in putting academic ideas into words for others.

- Make sure that students know that their sharing should (a) help them to build up their big idea(s) in their own minds and (b) help their listeners to clarify and support their idea(s). After sharing in a pair-share, the ideas in both students' own minds should be clearer and/or stronger from both sharing and listening.

- Create prompts that push students to build up ideas and share with others how they do this building (e.g., "Share some good evidence that you found for the theme of 'Do the right thing even if you don't want to'." "Share the criteria that you used for deciding whether or not the history book should include this account of the event." "Share both of your methods for solving this problem and how they connect to one another." "Describe and act out the water cycle to your partner.").

Requires and Helps Students to Clarify and Support

- Before the pair-share, have students quickly write down notes, a paragraph, or picture to prepare them to share their ideas as clearly and strongly as possible. They can then refer to notes and pictures (e.g., visual organizers) while they share, but they cannot read full sentences from any of their writing unless they are using a quotation from a text to support or clarify what they are saying.

- Partway through sharing (or after), have the speaker pause and say something like "Okay, take some notes and ask me a question that you really need or want to know." Some teachers stop the pair-shares and raise up colored cards to prompt listeners to ask either clarify or support questions.

- Model some of the language that students can use to clarify or support their ideas. For example, if they are sharing a hypothesis about a science demonstration that they just observed, you can model language such as "Because I noticed that ...., I think that ..., and I believe that it was caused by..." or "I think the theme was ... because it said on page 14 that she..." "A lot of people think that courage just means..., but I think, based on this text, that it also means...because..."

- Give A and B different texts or different parts of the same text that they share with one another.

- Have A and B answer different but related questions about the same topic ("Where does the energy in food come from?" "How does the energy in food get to our cells?").

- Tell A and B to share different answers to a question that has multiple possible answers—for example, "What is an important theme in this story?" "What is your opinion of..." "How can we solve this problem?" Tell one partner to start, and then have the second partner share a different idea. You can even bring up the idea of playing devil's advocate to make the pair-share more interesting.

- Alternate who starts (A or B) each time they share in pairs.

- Have students engage in two or more pair-shares in succession in which they improve how and what they say each time they share. See the Stronger and Clearer Each Time activities description in the first Going Deeper section, which follows the Classroom Example section.

- Use Transition Improv activities in which students, in pairs, cue one each other to describe two different ideas or claims. One is the director and the other is the speaker. See the second Going Deeper section for a description of these activities.

CLASSROOM EXAMPLE: Enhancing Pair-Shares in Fourth-Grade Science

In both versions, students had read a text on energy, and then they were going to use the information to do some of the real-life explorations described in the text, with the goal of better understanding how energy can be converted from one form to another. Notice how the two versions differ in how the teacher addresses typical challenges in students' speaking during think-pair-shares.

Original version. The teacher planned to put the standard on energy conversion (Next Generation Science Standards [NGSS] standard 4-PS3-4) up front and have students read it aloud. Then, after reading the text aloud to students, the teacher planned to have them turn to their partners to tell them the main idea of the text that they just read and how the conversion can be useful to people. Students would need to take notes on what their partners said in order to write the ideas down in their science journals, which they would turn in to get points. She planned to monitor student pair-shares to see if there were any misconceptions or questions.

Enhanced version. The teacher began the lesson by saying, "You and your partner are two scientists looking for ways to capture energy in cars while braking or going down hills. Each of you will read one of two different texts on energy conversion (a passage from the textbook and an article from the internet). Then you will share with a partner what you have learned from your text to come up with some ideas."

"Now, in your pair-shares, I want you to avoid several things I have seen over the years. First, don't just say one or two sentences and then expect your partner to do most of the talking. I will give a certain amount of time for each of you to talk, and I want you to fill up the entire time. Second, your partner can and should help you by asking what something means or for an example to keep you talking and building up the text summary that they need. Third, speak as clearly and accurately as possible to build up your text's ideas in your partner's mind—ideas that will help you both to come up with scientist solutions to our question about converting energy in cars. Use your voice and your hands to communicate as well as possible. And it's important to make sure your partner is understanding, which means reading your partner's facial expressions to see if there is any confusion at all, repeating anything that you think is new or complicated, and maybe using drawings, if necessary." Students then engaged in the pair-shares, and the teacher monitored the interactions to help students deepen and apply their ideas about the text.

GOING DEEPER: Stronger and Clearer Each Time Activities

In Stronger and Clearer Each Time activities, students engage in successive pair-shares on the same topic with the goal of improving students' ideas and language use each time they share. You can have students get into face-to-face lines, which helps you structure who talks with whom and speeds things up a bit. Students can also write down their idea before and after the paired inter-actions. You can have students work on a wide range of interpersonal communication skills, such as clarifying, using nonverbal communication, validating the ideas of others, and so on. Here is the basic procedure:

1. Pair students. A good pairing strategy is facing conversation lines that you call Line A and Line B. I recommend using smaller lines (e.g., three students facing three, four facing four).

2. Have Line A talk first. Give them between thirty and sixty seconds, depending on the topic and age. You can also have Line B students ask a support (or clarify) question to the partner (e.g., "Is there other evidence of that?"). I usually require this. Or, if their partner doesn't say much, listeners can even provide "idea seeds" that start with "What about…" Remind students that one of their jobs is to help their fellow students to talk more about what they are learning and to speak more effectively during the year about the ideas they are learning.

3. Then you can use a sound (e.g., one ding on a chime) to change turns in a partnership. Now A listens while B shares.

4. Then before having them switch to get new partners, have them tell one another, in just ten seconds apiece, what information or ideas from the partner that they liked and will take with them to share with the next partner share (e.g., "I really liked what you said about…because…"). They can also take notes between the two turns or before they switch to a new partner. They *should not* take notes while they are listening.

5. You can use different sound cues (two dings) for moving one of the lines (the first student goes down the middle to the end of his or her own line) so that all students shift and get a new partner. Line B students will share first this time. Before they start, remind them to borrow ideas and evidence (to make their ideas stronger) and language (to make their ideas clearer) from partners to make their ideas stronger and clearer for the next partner. If you don't model this and remind them often, they will tend to just say the same thing, or even less, each time.

6. After talking with and listening to three partners, have students write a postwrite response without looking at the prewrite. Then they can compare the two writings to see how the talking made a difference, and they can highlight the ideas and language that they borrowed from partners. You can look at pre- and postwrites to see what they might need to work on next.

The following is an edited example of a Stronger and Clearer Each Time activity that I observed in a sixth-grade English class. The teacher had just read aloud "Thank you, Ma'am" by Langston Hughes. The prompt was this: "At the end of the story, what was Roger thanking Mrs. Jones for, and how might what happened in the story end up changing him?" A is the focal student, P1 is Partner 1, P2 is Partner 2, etc., and T is the teacher. Look for ways in which A's response gets stronger and clearer each time.

A: I think that he was saying thank you because she was nice, even though he tried to steal her purse.

PI: What do you mean by nice?

A: So he tries to steal the purse, and she drags him to her house, and you think she's gonna punish him or call the police, but she gives him dinner and even money.

PI: What about changing him?

A: Oh yeah. I think he's gonna be a better person, like not steal anymore and maybe—

T: Okay, sorry to cut you off. The other person's turn now. Can you build on what you just heard? Yes. Go.

PI: I think that, too, that he was thanking her for not punishing him or calling the police—maybe even for doing like the opposite and to think that some people are good. Maybe he didn't have a mom or dad like that to sit down and have dinner with, or maybe he was like "Why would she do this for me?"

A: Yeah, and what about changing him?

PI: I think maybe he stops stealing and starts studying or working so he can, he can buy shoes with his own money.

T: Okay, take ten seconds apiece to tell your partner any ideas or evidence that they gave that you will add to your idea and share with your next partner.

A: I like what you said about the lady doing the opposite of what Roger expected—like it surprised him that people can be good.

PI: I like what you said about him wanting to become a better person.

T: Okay, now before you switch to a new partner, remember that your answer needs to be stronger and clearer than last time. (pause) Okay, switch! Folks in Line B begin.

P2: I think he is thanking her for being like a good mom that he doesn't have. Like when she asks him about anyone at home to tell him to wash his face and he says no. And for forgiving him for trying to steal from her. And she was like a stranger. Maybe a mom or

(Continued)

(Continued)

aunt would forgive him, but not a stranger. I wouldn't have done that for him. But I think he would change to not steal things anymore; maybe even forgive people.

A: Why wouldn't you do that?

P2: Maybe I would if I was Mrs. Jones, cuz she, I think, maybe wanted to have a son, or maybe wanted to help kids in the neighborhood.

T: Okay, Line A, go. You can use ideas from your first partnership and from the partner you just heard from.

A: I think he said thank you for a couple reasons. He was thanking her for not turning him in to the police. And I think he was thanking her for being like a mom he doesn't have, you know, for telling him to wash his face and for giving him a warm dinner and hot chocolate. And like you said, maybe he thanks her for showing him that strangers can be good people. And for giving him ten dollars to buy shoes. Maybe he was even thanking her for getting him to start changing to not steal and work for money. I don't know.

I included only two partnerships instead of three because of the length. However, notice how A's idea got stronger and clearer, even in just two turns. Also notice the prompting for clarification and the extra supporting evidence that Student A gets from his first two partners. Notice that this example had only one text, but the prompt was open enough to allow for different responses from different partners (i.e., for information gaps). Another option, if you think student answers might overlap too much, is giving out four different text excerpts on the topic, having groups of four with the different texts rotate partners, and having them refer to their texts when they share.

GOING DEEPER: Transition Improv Activities

Transition Improv activities are paired oral language activities in which one student, the *director*, directs the other student, the *speaker*, to go back and forth describing and building up two opposing sides of a topic. It helps students to build speaking skills, sharpen their thinking about the topic, beef up content learning, and support them in using appropriate transitions for communicating ideas. It takes little preparation and is done easily in pairs. In the most common Transition Improv activity, the pro-con, the speakers need to describe and build up the pro side and con side of a topic as much as possible. Here is the procedure:

1. You can give them a topic from a current text or lesson, the talker can choose it from a list, or the talker can opt to have the director choose it. It's a good idea to give students some practice with more common topics such as shopping, camping, cars, cell phones, the Internet, school, video games, social media, etc. When they seem comfortable with the format, you can move to more lesson-focused topics such as Thomas Jefferson, the use of violence to fight for freedom, technology, democracy, communism, nuclear power, Napoleon, the sun, stem cell research, etc.

2. Remind directors that they need to listen carefully so that when their speakers have finished arguing the pros and cons of each side, they can infer which side the speaker really leans toward.

3. The director starts the conversation by saying the topic and then "Pro!"

4. The speaker comes up with multiple sentences about a positive aspect of the topic for twenty seconds or so, using any examples or evidence he or she can think of to strengthen this side. At an appropriate time, the director then says, "Con!" and the same speaker must start the con turn with an academic transition (e.g., however, on the other hand, yet, then again). They can't say nothing, and they can't start with the word *but* because it's so commonly used already.

5. The director should listen well, making eye contact, nodding, and adopting a posture that shows interest. The director should give time for the speaker to talk. There might be some awkward silences at times. These are okay because they allow the speaker some time to think. The director shouldn't switch to the other side too soon (e.g., after one sentence). For example, if a speaker starts off a con turn with "Watching TV messes with your brain" and stops, the director should wait a few seconds, indicating that one sentence isn't enough. If the speaker still doesn't talk more, the director can do one of three things: (1) prompt for support with evidence or examples (e.g., "Can you give examples of the bad things that happen to your brain?"), (2) prompt the speaker for clarification (e.g., "What do you mean 'mess with your brain'?"), or (3) if the speaker is out of ideas, provide idea seeds that the speaker can elaborate on in order to help him or her build up each side even more (e.g., "What about the article that said TV watchers do worse on tests?").

6. The director switches the speaker back and forth several times to get three pro turns and three con turns.

7. Afterward, the teacher prompts the directors to say to their speakers, "I think you leaned on the side of ... because you ..." The director can use the quantity and/or quality of reasons and examples for one side versus the other, as well as any movement or prosodic cues ("because your face lit up and you moved your hands a lot more when you talked about...").

8. Then students switch roles and switch topics. Optionally, you can have them use the same topic, but you should give them different articles or information beforehand so that there is an information gap and more authentic communication. An advantage is that they build up both sides of a topic even more.

Other Transition Improv activities, all of which have students flipping back and forth between opposing ideas and using transitions to do so, include the following:

- For-against (e.g., "Reintroducing wolves into Yellowstone National Park . . . For!")

- Similar-different (e.g., "World War I and World War II... Similar!"),

- Two perspectives (e.g., Montag! ...Beatty! Jefferson!...Hamilton!)

 ## Enhanced Jigsaws

Jigsaws can provide students with a way to develop their idea-building skills. In many jigsaws happening in schools, students are teamed up in groups to become "experts" on a particular text that other expert groups are not reading. This tends to create helpful information gaps. A popular way to structure this activity is by giving students matrices or charts that need to be filled in with information from their text. Expert groups fill in one row or column that they then share with experts on other rows or columns when they return to their "home" groups.

While such activities do create information gaps and thus can provide some sense of purpose, the purpose is often just to fill in the chart rather than to understand and communicate the material. I have seen too many jigsaws in which students copied from the text onto their papers and then just passed their papers around to be copied from in the home group, with minimal talk. As you will see by the enhancements in the procedure, there is much more they can do to deepen their communication and engagement.

- Remind students that the purpose of the jigsaw activity is to help others and be helped by others to build up ideas that will help everyone excel in their final tasks and build up ideas that they will use in life. They can do this most effectively by (a) speaking clearly and completely as an expert on the topic would speak and (b) listening attentively in home groups to key points and taking notes on the information that they will need for their final tasks.

- Let students choose a graphic organizer that they think will work best for them to keep track of the key information that they will need. Rather than a matrix, they might choose to use and keep adding to a Venn diagram, semantic map, T-chart, outline, flowchart, argument balance scale, idea-building blueprint (see Chapter 2 or the online appendix), and so forth.

- Have expert and/or home groups create podcasts, videos, or other products that challenge students to describe the ideas they are building up in more robust and visible ways. For example, an expert group might work together to create a podcast or video on their topic that they record and then play for their home group. The home group members can then take notes while listening, ask questions, and even give feedback on how to improve the podcast or video.

Requires and Helps Students to Clarify and Support

- Have expert groups discuss not only *what* they will share in home groups but also *how* they will most clearly and strongly communicate the key information to their peers in their home groups. Have them discuss what they think their home groups will want and need most as well as how best to help them take notes and remember the information to be shared. They can also use a variation of Figure 5.1 for this.

- Within the expert groups, have students rehearse twice in pairs what they will say when they present to home groups. For the first partnership, the presenter can use notes. For sharing with the second partner, the presenter doesn't use notes. For each practice run, the listener asks questions and provides feedback on clarity and support and reminds the person presenting of any content or evidence that should be included to make the idea stronger.

- Encourage students to develop the skill of speaking in paragraphs. This skill is described in the next Going Deeper section.

- Challenge students to not use notes when they share information with their home groups. They can hand their notes to another home group member who can remind them of anything they forget to share. Ask home group listeners to try to come up with at least one authentic clarify or support question each time a member shares. If the presenter doesn't know the answer, they can all decide if it's valuable enough to write down and look up later.

- After the home group presentations, have students discuss as a group how to fill in a visual organizer that shows the building up of ideas (e.g., on an idea-building blueprint [see Chapter 2 or the online appendix]). This allows students, after listening, to process what they heard and how it can help them construct ideas that they will use beyond the jigsaw.

- Hold a whole-class discussion to further synthesize, build, clarify, and support ideas that students discussed in their expert and home groups. As you circulate and listen in on group presentations, you might hear some (a) highly useful insights that the whole class could benefit from and (b) misconceptions that need to be corrected and clarified.

- In math, give each expert group a different problem to solve, which they need to present and explain to home groups. Then, after all have presented, they discuss how the problems help them to build up one or more key ideas about how math works.

CLASSROOM EXAMPLE: Enhancing a Jigsaw in Third-Grade Social Studies

Students had been learning about heroes of the Civil War era. This jigsaw activity focused on understanding the qualities that make a person a hero. Look for ways in which the enhanced version of this jigsaw activity pushes students to improve what they say and how they say it.

Original version. The teacher planned to start with this question: "Tell me who your heroes are." Students would respond by listing family members, singers, actors, and athletes. Then the teacher would say, "Why are they heroes? That's what we will look at today: their qualities, words, and actions that make them heroes. We will read about four different heroes in our nation's history: Harriet Tubman, Rosa Parks, Abraham Lincoln, and Frederick Douglass. We will do a jigsaw in which you will read about one person and hear from others about the other people." She would hand out a worksheet with a table where they could record what they learned. She would say, "Here is the table you will fill in with four rows for the four people and three columns for their qualities, actions, and words. After you fill in your expert row, you will meet in home groups and teach the others about the hero you read about."

Enhanced version. The teacher started off with "Today we will look at what makes a person a hero. Many of you know about superheroes. Besides having special powers, what makes them heroes?" Students shared ideas such as helping others, stopping bad people, etc. "Do you have any heroes? Share with a partner who and why they are heroes to you." After the students shared with their partners and then shared in a brief whole-class share-out, the teacher continued, "Okay. Let's see if some of those reasons you just mentioned are found in the people we will learn about today. At the end of the day I want you to build up an idea of the qualities that heroes should have, and I want you to think about how we can be a class of heroes now and in the future."

Students broke into eight expert groups of four. She let each group choose a way of taking notes. One group chose a semantic map with Hero in the middle box and put Actions, Words, and Qualities in circles around the box. The expert groups then read one of the four texts and filled in their graphic organizers. She asked expert members to pair up and practice what they would later say in their home groups and asked listening partners to push for clarity and support (e.g., "What does *brave* mean?" "What's an example of not being selfish?") and provide suggestions. Then students went to their home groups to present. The teacher encouraged listeners to try to get as much information from each expert as they could—by listening—in order to build up their ideas about heroes. She also encouraged the speakers to use any actions, drama, visuals, and examples that made the mini presentation stronger and clearer.

GOING DEEPER: Speaking in Paragraphs

This practice, which can fit within many speaking activities, is a way to help students organize information, think, and speak in paragraph-shaped ways. That is, it cultivates the habit of grouping related ideas and leading off with a topic sentence. This not only improves their oral communication but also bulks up their reading and writing skills. The practice develops students' abilities to put an idea into a strong topic sentence and then clarify and support it with additional sentences. Students learn that topic sentences tend to be more general and abstract (e.g., "We should lower the voting age." "The circulatory system carries oxygen and nutrients to the body's cells."), while the clarifying and supporting sentences describe necessary details and evidence.

An easy way to introduce the activity is with questions that ask for opinions and supporting facts or reasons. Share some nonexamples by starting off with evidence or details without a topic sentence. You can also share a topic sentence without clarifying or supporting sentences. Then share some good sample responses, and have students describe which were clearer and why.

Here are some steps to foster this practice:

1. Prepare prompts or questions (or better yet, choose questions that students have generated) for students to answer. These questions should be big enough for paragraph-length answers. This means answers with more than a few words but not so big as to demand a full-blown essay. The questions should allow the responder to come up with a topic sentence and then support and clarify it with other sentences (e.g., "How did Cassie change in the novel?" "What was one reason people immigrated at the turn of the century?" "What is a fraction?" "What causes the tides?").

2. After seeing or hearing a question, give students time to think, without writing anything down. If they struggle, they can draw or jot down short notes (not sentences) before talking. Then they should cover these up before talking.

3. They come up with a first (topic) sentence and follow it with two to eight other sentences to support it or clarify it. A conclusion sentence is optional. If needed, listeners can prompt for additional clarifications or support.

For example, in a science jigsaw activity, in expert groups students had read different texts to answer this question: "What are reasons for eating healthy food?" After switching back into home groups, the first student said, "We should eat healthy food because you can get sick if you don't. Your body needs a bunch of different nutrients and vitamins and protein to stay healthy and fight off sickness. If all you eat is sugar and fat, you miss out on vitamins and protein that cells need. And if you eat too much, you can become overweight. This can cause more sicknesses and clog up your arteries. This can give you a heart attack. So we should eat healthy foods."

It helps students think and speak in paragraphs, as often as possible, in different lesson activities such as answering questions in whole-class discussions, pair-shares, group projects, presentations, and gallery walks.

In some gallery walks, the teacher puts up posters with important (or mysterious) images around the room and has groups of students go around and respond in some way to them. In other gallery walks, groups of students create something (e.g., a poster) that they put up around the room. Some teachers have students form small groups (or just walk around on their own) and view the posters, sometimes writing comments on a separate posted sheet or on sticky notes right on the poster. Other teachers have one or two group members stay at their poster to explain it and teach the concept to others, while the other group members go around and become mini audiences for the other groups' mini presentations. Some teachers have the group present their ideas to the rest of the class as they all walk around to each poster.

Here are some suggestions for enhancing gallery walk activities even more in order to increase authentic communication.

Requires and Helps Students to Purposefully Build Ideas

- Create a purpose for which the different posters and short presentations help the audience to build up disciplinary ideas. They might record a podcast on the topic for a specific audience, do a radio interview, design a product, produce a documentary, write an article for a local newspaper, or create a final poster that informs the public of an issue.

- As students are presenting their ideas, have listeners take notes or fill in an organizer with information that will be useful to them for their eventual or ongoing performance task or project. They then can compare notes with others to make sure they got it all.

- Use the model in Figure 5.1 as an initial guide to help students prepare their gallery presentations, and you can work with students to create their own organizers and posters to scaffold the development of the idea that they will share.

Requires and Helps Students to Clarify and Support

- Before presenting their posters, students practice what they will say with their own group members who ask clarifying and supporting questions that the eventual listeners might ask. This helps the presenter(s) prepare to deliver a clear and strong presentation.

- Before the gallery walk, have students record their presentations using devices, and then listen to them for ways to improve them. You can also have them record their live gallery walk presentations for self- and teacher feedback. They can use checklists and rubrics as they listen or watch.

- Before the gallery walk, remind students to practice speaking in paragraphs (see the first Going Deeper section in this chapter). Remind them that paragraphs are the best way to help their listeners organize and remember the important information that they listen to.

- During the gallery walk presentations, have listeners prompt the presenter to clarify and support ideas with examples and evidence. Encourage them to validate ("Wow, that's interesting!") throughout and to ask questions such as "I need to know more about…" "Which evidence do you think is strongest, and why?" "What did your group think that (term) meant/means?"

- After listening and before moving to the next presentation, listeners can give the presenter kudos for what he or she did well and suggestions for improving the presentation for the next group of listeners. Kudos might include saying things such as "Great job…! I really liked how you …" "Keep … in your next presentation." "Thank you! I felt like you really cared that we learn this stuff." Suggestions would include recommending using more gestures, adding something to the poster, speaking in paragraphs, being louder to emphasize key points, making eye contact with all of us, etc.

Requires and Helps Students to Fill Information Gaps

- Structure it so groups have different topics that don't overlap too much but at the same time fit together enough to help all students build up important concepts by listening to all of the poster presentations. For example, each team might focus on a different aspect of the culture or history of a certain group of people, and in the end they put the information together to complete their projects.

- Have each member of one group pair up with each member of another group to share their posters in pairs (instead of having just one person from group share and a whole group listen). This can help maximize the amount of focused speaking and listening that students engage in.

- As students listen to each presenter, have them try to think of at least one thing that they really want to know about the topic, especially the information that will help them accomplish the larger purpose, task, or project. They can put this question on a card that you collect. Alternate who gets to ask for this information at the end of each presentation so that it's not just the same student asking each time. The presenter can also respond with something like "That's an interesting question. How will it help you with your final project?"

- If the activity spans two or more days, have students practice explaining their ideas and posters (they can make a small copy of it) to parents or others at home as part of their homework. The listeners at home ask clarifying questions and can write down their understanding of the concept on the student's homework page (or audio-record it).

CLASSROOM EXAMPLE: Enhancing a Gallery Walk in Fifth-Grade History

The gallery walk activity in this lesson is part of a unit on the development of the government in the early years of the United States. Notice how the activity procedures are framed and presented differently in the two versions in order to expand students' abilities to speak about academic topics.

Original version. The teacher had chosen eight documents to study: (1) the Magna Carta, (2) the Mayflower Compact, (3) the Virginia Plan, (4) *Common Sense* (by Thomas Paine), (5) the Declaration of Independence, (6) the Articles of Confederation, (7) the Constitution, and (8) the Bill of Rights. She planned on forming eight groups of students, each of which would focus on one of the documents, create a poster, and then share the key information with others in a gallery walk activity on Friday. Students would look at the original texts, with portions of them highlighted by the teacher, and students would look at summaries of them as well. The teacher planned to tell students that, after the gallery walk, they would need to write an essay that brings in ideas from at least four of the documents. The essay would focus on what students thought were the most important principles that the original framers of government wanted to foster.

Enhanced version. The teacher started the week with this question: "If you wanted to form a new government, what would it look like? How might it function? How will you make decisions? Why?" The teacher explained that these were the types of questions that the early colonies faced after gaining independence from Great Britain. She said, "We will work as a class to look at eight different documents that helped the early U.S. leaders establish a government. In groups you will focus on one document, and you will share your research with others in a gallery walk on Friday. Your main focus will be looking for the key ideas about government and how a country should run, with a focus on the ideas and principles that the Founders wanted to continue into the future. These key ideas might involve valuing human rights, defining the role of state and federal government, clarifying the power of the president, outlining the checks and balances between different branches of the government, etc. I want your group to create a poster that shows a summary of your document, why it was written, how it was eventually used, its key ideas or principles, and your collective opinion of its value and importance." You will use your information and the information from other groups to help you come up with a plan for your new government.

After several days of research, students finished up the posters and practiced in their own groups what they would say the next day to others. Group members gave feedback as each member rehearsed to improve the clarity and strength of the presentation. On Friday, the teacher said, "Okay, Member A in each group will stay and teach your own poster for two rotations. Then Member B for the next two, and so on. You will take notes as you listen to other poster presentations. These notes will help you to improve your final plans. As you listen to a person present, each person needs to ask at least one clarifying or justifying question. For example, if a presenter says, 'They wanted freedom of religion,' you can ask what that means or why it's important. The more information you get, the better. Remember that you're building up the idea of what the Founders wanted government to look like and do for the new nation along with your opinion of how well it worked. And these ideas will help you create your new government plan."

The teacher reminded presenters that the information they would share is vital for helping their listeners to build up their ideas and improve their plans. Presenters shared for several minutes and allowed for questions at the end. The teacher reminded the presenters that they should use the questions and feedback from this presentation to improve subsequent presentations.

 ## Enhanced Shared Problem Solving in Math

This activity includes any type of task in which students are asked to use multiple sentences and connectors to describe the procedures for solving a math problem, including the reasoning that supports those procedures. Well-known activities such as number talks and math talks could fit into this category as well as when students teach others how they solved a problem in front of the whole class, in pairs, and in small groups. Here are some suggestions for increasing the authentic communication of such activities.

- Remind students that all problem solving is meant to help them think about how math works. Tell students, after they describe the procedures, to share an idea or concept for how math works, such as a claim, conjecture, or generalization that was sparked by solving this and similar problems Here is a sample generalization: "Solving this type of problem reminds me that no matter what shape the triangle has, its angles add up to 180 degrees. And we can use that to solve other problems with triangles and their angles.")

- Have students use the math idea-building blueprint (see Chapter 2 or the online appendix) to help them organize the building blocks for their big ideas after they solve and create problems.

- Assign more robust presentation-based projects (e.g., at the end of a unit) that focus on students orally describing a big idea that they have learned in the unit as a result of solving problems, creating their own problems, and discussing how math works with others.

- Encourage speakers to practice justifying each procedural decision so that listeners will come away with a clear picture of their reasoning. Have listeners ask speakers to support each statement about each procedure used (e.g., "Why did you divide right then?")

- Take "big idea breaks" in which you have pairs practice describing to one another their evolving big ideas, using words, visuals, gestures, and examples. Have the partners provide feedback on the idea's clarity and support. When listening and providing feedback, partners can ask themselves questions such as "Is my partner's idea clear and strong enough to convince me, others, and the teacher that he or she knows this concept well?"

- Tell all students that they need to listen well to one another because they will need to refer to the procedures and reasoning of their peer speakers to build up their own ideas and complete their final tasks and products.

- As students work on problems (e.g., a launch problem), observe their problem-solving methods and then have some students with unique methods present to the larger group. Then have students discuss the connections between two or more solution methods.

- Give pairs of students different problems, and then have them present the problems, their solution methods, justification of procedures, and mathematical ideas that the problems show. Use the information gap math cards activity, described in the next Going Deeper section in this chapter.

The goal in both versions was to give students opportunities to share their thinking about how to solve and create problems involving the addition and subtraction of angles and degrees. Notice how the enhanced version pushes students to justify their methods and work to articulate their mathematical thinking to others.

Original version. The teacher planned to model how to figure out the measures of angles and solve problems. She would use a problem about a rotating sprinkler on a circular field by presenting the following situation: A farmer planted crops on a circular area of land. Her sprinkler was anchored in the center and rotated around to give water to the entire area. But one day, the sprinkler got stuck after moving 135 degrees around. How many degrees were left unwatered? The teacher planned to put the students into groups of four to work on the problem. Then one person from each group would present their solution method to the rest of the class.

Enhanced version. The teacher started off by presenting several real-world examples of situations that required an understanding of angles and degrees (clocks, circus tents, architecture). The teacher then paused to remind students that the problems that they would do were meant to help them build up their ideas about angles, how to show them, and how to solve problems with them. She gave each pair one of two different problems: the sprinkler problem and a similar problem on longitude. She told the pairs to do two things: (1) solve the problem and (2) practice how they would teach it to another person who hasn't yet solved it. After each one got some practice time, the pairs broke up and students paired up this time with someone who did the *other* problem. They then taught each other how to do their respective problems. If the partner who was teaching at the moment didn't justify procedures, then the listener asked why. The teacher then gave students different real-world scenarios to create their own problems that they would later trade with other students.

When both were done, they worked together in a group of four to build up a mathematical idea that they thought the problems were meant to teach. The teacher had them briefly practice with a partner what they would say if the principal came in and asked them what they were learning. The teacher then had several students explain their methods and share their evolving ideas about angles to the whole class. For example, one student said, "You can solve a lot of these problems when you know that all the degrees in a circle are 360. You can add 'em up or subtract from 360, like in the sprinkler problem or the one we made up about the race car. It went around one quarter of the track, that was 90 degrees, so it had 270 to go. All the angles in a circle add up to 360…"

GOING DEEPER: Information Gap Math Cards Activity

In this activity, you or your students create A and B cards. Card A has the word problem without the numbers or other visual information (shapes, tables, graphs, diagrams), which you put on Card B, the data card. Students need to bridge the information gap by orally exchanging information. They should sit side by side to work together, but they shouldn't show or read their cards to each other. Here is the procedure:

1. Partner A reads the A card silently and thinks about what information is needed to solve it. Partner B also silently reads the data card.

2. Partner A paraphrases the problem (but doesn't read it out loud) to Partner B, who asks clarifying questions and then paraphrases the problem for A. The goal in this step is for both students to have a shared understanding of the problem.

3. Partner A then asks B for a piece of specific information that is needed to solve the problem (e.g., a quantity such as how many gallons does the tank hold).

4. If Partner A asks for something and does not automatically justify why it's needed, Partner B should ask for justification before telling A the information (e.g., "Why do you need that information?"). B should ask for justification even if B already assumes he or she knows why A is asking for the information.

5. Partner A explains why he or she needs it, and B decides if the justification is strong and clear enough to tell the information to A. For all the students with A cards you can provide some language support with more complex

sentences such as "In order to …, I need…" "Because I need to …, I need to know…" or "Without that information, I can't…" Also, if A doesn't ask for the information on Card B, or B doesn't have the information, or A simply gets stuck at some point, Student B can say something like "I don't have that, but I do have ____. Would that help you? How?"

6. Partner A tries to solve the problem and explains his or her procedures as B observes and asks why when appropriate. Partner B can also help when Partner A wants or needs it.

7. Finally, both students talk to figure out how this problem and its solution methods are examples of one or more important mathematical ideas that they are supposed to learn.

8. *Optionally,* students work together to write a similar, yet even more interesting, problem. This "reverse engineering" of a problem further builds up their conceptual understandings. Think about how much teachers learn by coming up with good problems.

Here is an example of A and B cards in a fifth-grade math class:

A month ago the garden center delivered some bags of soil to our school for the garden. At the end of the month, there was some soil left in the second and third bags. How much soil was used during the month?	• Three bags were delivered. • Each bag started with 5 ½ pounds. • 1st bag = none left in it • 2nd bag = ¾ lb. left in it • 3rd bag = 2 ¼ lb. left in it

Figure 5.2 Sample Information Gap Math Cards

Here is a portion of an interaction between two students who were using these cards:

A: The problem is we got, the school, got some soil last month and used some of it up. There is soil left in the second and third bags, but I don't know how much. It asks how much soil we used.

B: So the problem is about bags of soil. You used up the first one, I think, and there is some left in the other two bags. And you gotta find out how much you used up. Right?

A: Right. So I need to know how many bags. I think three, right?

B: Why do you need to know that?

A: Because it says second and third, but maybe there were more, and I need it to know cuz if a fourth bag was used, that's more.

B: Okay. Yeah. Three.

A: And how much was left in the second bag?

B: Why do you need to know that?

A: To subtract it.

B: From what?

A: From the total. Like if I know how much total was in them to start, then I subtract what's left, right?

B: Okay. There's ¾ of a pound left in it.

A: And the third bag?

B: 2 ¼ pounds

A: So now, let's see. I still need the totals, like for each bag. What did they start with?

B: Why do you need to know that?

A: Like I said, to subtract them from it. I mean, yeah, to subtract like the ¾ pound from the total that was in the bag.

B: Okay. Each bag started off with 5 ½ pounds.

A: Thanks. Now I do 5 ½ minus ¾, wait, I gotta borrow from the big number.

B: What do you mean?

A: The ½ isn't enough, so I gotta take ½ from the 5; now it's 4. See? And now it's ½ minus ¾, so it's big enough. So 3 minus 3 is 0.

B: Wait, you have to have the same number on the bottom, remember?

A: Oh yeah. So ½ times ½ is ⁶⁄₄, so that's better. ⁶⁄₄ minus ¾ is ¾.
So 4 ¾ …

Notice how this structured interaction activity fostered a lot of productive processing of content and language—more so than many typical paired interactions that focus on problem solving. You can give student pairs two different problems to work on, one after the other, so that they can each play the roles of Student A and Student B.

SUMMARY

Speaking is a great way to see what students are thinking and learning. But even more than that, it is a powerful way to learn because when students are communicating orally to others, they are pushing their minds to organize, clarify, and strengthen their evolving ideas. In addition, purposeful speaking about academic topics fosters students' sense of voice, agency, and academic identity. Even though it gets loud and some students do get off task when they talk, we must continue to provide and nurture opportunities for extended speaking because, in many ways, their future learning, relationships, and success in the world will depend on it.

REFLECTION QUESTIONS

1. Think of a common activity in your lessons that either intentionally develops speaking or depends a lot on speaking. How authentic is it? How strong are the three features of authentic communication? How might it be enhanced?

2. In what ways can speaking help your students learn more effectively?

3. How can you formatively assess students' speaking (including tools, peer assessment, and self-assessment)?

AUTHENTIC WRITING

I suggest that we're currently wasting a lot of time by giving unreal writing tasks in our classrooms . . . You and I don't engage in meaningless writing exercises in real life—we're far too busy doing the real thing.

—Mem Fox (1993)

A common question from teachers is "How can I improve my students' scores on writing assessments?" But what we should be asking is "How can I help my students communicate as effectively as possible in their writing?" One way is to get our students to be asking, "How can I communicate to my readers as effectively as possible?" And the question undergirding both of these is "How can we increase the authenticity of writing and its learning power in every classroom?" This is the focus of this chapter.

There are several challenges to address when trying to increase the authenticity of writing in school. First, many students think that the sole purpose of writing is to get points or a letter grade. They haven't learned that one writes to communicate ideas and to influence, inform, and build up ideas in readers' minds. Second, standards, schools, and curriculums have pushed rigid "this is how you have to write to get your points" approaches for many years. Third, many students don't think they have ideas to share or that they are good writers. And fourth, most students, when they read a well-written text, don't see how much effort and editing went into it.

When we increase the authentic communication in writing activities and tasks, students tend to be more motivated to go beyond the bare minimum. They work harder to put their ideas into organized sentences, to revise, to edit, and to do what they can to help readers understand their writing. We might provide scaffolds, checklists, and rubrics, but all of these should serve the primary purpose of improving how the writing communicates to others.

Figure 6.1, which is very similar to Figure 5.1 in the last chapter, shows a model for helping students express ideas to others in writing, along with other forms of representation that need to be interpreted visually. You start with the purpose (WHY) in the first box. Then in Box 2 you build up an idea in the writing (WHAT) that will serve the purpose in Box 1. You focus on making the idea as strong as possible with evidence, examples, and reasoning. Then in Box 3 you think about HOW to most clearly express the idea. There are many considerations—all of which depend on what your readers need and want.

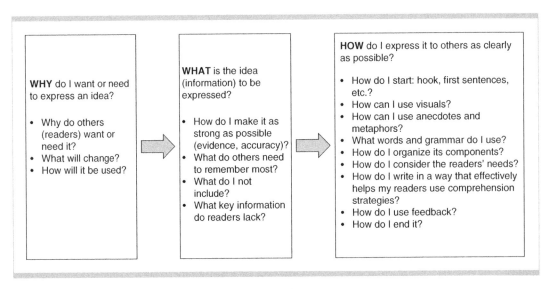

Figure 6.1   Model for Writing and/or Representing Ideas

The classroom is fertile ground for improving writing skills because there are so many readers who can give a writer feedback on how well his or her writing is communicating an idea. Yet this ground is often neglected. This is because in many classrooms students revise and edit individually. Instead of guessing if their writing will communicate well to readers, students can have other students read their writing and tell them directly what works and what needs to improve. But students doing the peer editing and revising must have a communication mindset, not a "I'm helping you get a better score for when you turn this into the teacher" mindset.

MAXIMIZING CLARITY AND STRENGTH IN WRITING

As students work on developing the specific features of different writing genres, they may want to organize and extend their questioning by using the following list.

- *Purpose:* Why am I writing this? How can I best accomplish my purpose through writing?

- *Audience:* What do my readers need to know?

- *Point of view:* What point of view will best help my readers understand the idea?

- *Introduction:* How can I best let readers know what the writing is about? What will hook my readers in the most?

- *Evidence:* Do I need to use stronger evidence than what I currently have? Will the reader be convinced by this? Why? Do I need to go back to the text? How can I best explain how the evidence supports the main idea?

- *Clarity:* I think I need to clarify what _____ means in this paragraph. I bet the reader would ask about…

- *Figurative language:* How can I use similes, metaphors, or analogies to make my complex ideas more understandable?

- *Genre:* What genre will best communicate my idea (story, poem, letter, interview, etc.)?

- *Word choice:* Which words will my audience understand the most?

- *Topic sentences:* Do the topic sentences for each paragraph communicate the paragraphs' ideas clearly?

- *Sentence variation:* Do my sentences vary enough so that my readers will not be bored with simple sentence and not be overwhelmed with too many long and complex sentences?

(Continued)

(Continued)

- *Grammar:* Does grammar get in the way of readers' understanding? Do verb tenses match their subjects? Do I make sure not to mix past and present tenses? Do I use complete sentences? If I do use a sentence fragment, do I do it for effect?

- *Paragraphs:* Do I break subideas into paragraphs to help the reader chunk information?

- *Conclusion:* How can I end this with a powerful summary or reminder of the issue?

As you can see, these questions and thoughts tend to get writers to push themselves for more clarity and support during writing. Effective writers have the habit of thinking about these things before and during writing. But remember, just telling students to ask the questions, giving points for responding to them, or putting them up on a wall isn't enough. Instead, consider which ones your students need to focus on the most and how you might encourage students to engage in this thinking as they write. I have seen teachers put them into checklists and then have students listen to partners for similar thoughts as they talk through their writing process. Other teachers model their writing aloud and have students listen for these thoughts and questions during the modeling.

So get to know your students' needs, and weave these focuses and questions into the enhancements that you make to your writing instruction. Some examples of this weaving and enhancements are found in the following section.

AUTHENTIC WRITING ACTIVITIES

Here are four common writing activities with enhancements based on the three features of authentic communication. For many students an enormous objective, or mission, is to change their mindset about writing from that of being assessed to that of communicating ideas to others. A related mission is to help students to value their ideas enough to write them down for others and try different ways of expressing their ideas in writing. Schooling has trained too many students to think of writing as a chore that they are not good at, and the enhancements that follow attempt to change this type of thinking.

Similar to reading workshops, writing workshops typically start with a teacher mini lesson that covers an aspect of writing that the teacher wants students to practice in their workshop time. Students work on their own for large chunks of time as the teacher circulates to provide feedback and confer with individual students. If desired, the teacher can work with small groups of students on a skill, feature, or trait, which is a strategy that is often referred to as guided writing. Students can also confer with one another for peer editing and feedback. Usually, there is a combination of conferencing, drafting, revising, illustrating, final editing, and publishing. (There are plenty of resources out there on writing or writer's workshops if you want more information.) Here are some enhancements that focus on increasing the authenticity of the communication in different parts of the activity.

Requires and Helps Students to Purposefully Build Ideas

- Express to students your fervent desire for them to realize that their ideas are valuable and worth communicating in writing. This is a foundation for being motivated to do the work needed for effective writing. If students don't value their own ideas or think that potential readers don't want or need to read their ideas, they won't work as hard to make their ideas as clear and strong as possible. Emphasize that their writing will inform, influence, and change the minds and hearts of readers. (And the prompt should reflect this emphasis too.)

- Let students choose a prewriting graphic organizer that they think will work best for them. Have them tell a partner their reasons for choosing the particular organizer.

- If there is argumentation (typically starting around Grade 3, though I have seen this done well in Grades 1 and 2), students should also build up a claim with evidence and reasons, and then they should build up at least one solid counterclaim. Have them compare the two sides, and then explain how the claim that they choose has stronger reasoning and evidence.

- Interview younger students about what kinds of stories they like to read, and then write and illustrate a story for the student(s). (See the next Going Deeper section for a more complete description of this.)

- Emphasize that the purpose of a writing rubric (or checklist) is to help students push for improved clarity and support in order to communicate better. Have students use the rubric to remind them of what needs to be included in the writing in order to help readers understand their important ideas.

- Give students a good chunk of time to talk through what they plan to write in order to get any feedback on what clarification or support might be needed by potential readers. Have students meet with different partners at different stages of writing to give feedback that pushes one another to clarify and strengthen ideas. They can look at the rubric to help them provide feedback.

- When peer editing, have peer editors use two colors of pen or pencil to show clarifying and supporting feedback when they write comments on the papers or sticky notes.

Requires and Helps Students to Fill Information Gaps

- Have students go through their notes and drafts to take things out that the reader will likely already know. Remind them that they don't want their readers saying "duh!" while reading their writings.

- As you confer with students, ask them to include information that you don't know. Many students think that that they need to include information that they have learned in order to prove to you that they know it. But it's not a test; it's a chance for them to make a difference in your mind and in other readers' minds.

- As you (and fellow students) confer with an author, suggest the use of words and syntax that are new to them in order to vary their uses of language. For example, you might have them combine simple sentences in spots so that the message doesn't sound so choppy.

- Give students a purpose for transforming one text into a different type of text or genre, such as a textbook chapter into a newspaper article, a biography into a poster, a story into a poem, an article into an interview, a painting into a story, a story into a play. The new form should emphasize and clarify key information from the original form, ideally in ways that communicate it better, more clearly, and more memorably for readers.

In both versions, students need to engage in writing workshop work to write a well-developed paragraph in response to their reading of *Tuck Everlasting* (Babbitt, 1975). They need to focus on developing and describing an important theme in the story. Notice how the enhanced version addresses ways to improve written communication by addressing the problems that happen when the features of a strong paragraph are not included.

Original version. The teacher had created a rubric that focused on the development of the idea, organization, word choice, linking words and phrases, sentence fluency, and conventions. She planned to model how to write a paragraph about a theme. She would start off the mini lesson by going over an anchor chart for paragraphs with a hamburger on it: The buns are the topic sentence and conclusion; the inner fixings are the supporting sentences. She would write a topic sentence and then write the other sentences with linking terms, which she would underline. Then she planned to tell students that she would be looking for good topic sentences and linking terms between sentences. After brainstorming ideas for themes from the book that they wanted to write about, students would write their drafts.

Enhanced version. The teacher started off the lesson with a brief review of how authors include themes in their stories to teach life lessons to readers. She also reminded them that writing is a powerful way to help other people understand their ideas, so they need to work hard to make their writing strong and clear for all who read it. Then she showed a sample nonmodel paragraph about a minor theme in *Tuck Everlasting* that had no topic sentence and no linking words between sentences. She read it to them and asked, "Did any of you think that you were having trouble building up an idea when you read this? (head nods) What do you think would help this paragraph communicate better?" After a few responses, she showed the same paragraph with a topic sentence and linking terms. She asked, "Why is this one better at communicating to us, the readers?"

After a brief discussion, she also went over the hamburger chart described in the original version, reinforcing the idea that all elements play a role in a paragraph, just as they do in a hamburger. She wrote her own paragraph to model how to include these features. She chose another theme and thought aloud as she wrote, saying, "I know I need to start my paragraph with a topic sentence so that the reader knows what the paragraph is about. So how about, 'One theme in the novel *Tuck Everlasting* is how important it is that we appreciate the time we have here.'" Then she wrote several other sentences that were connected with terms and phrases such as "The first part that shows this theme is..." "Another part that supports this theme is..." "Finally, ..." Then she had students take out their big idea journals in which they had been writing key ideas from texts they had been reading all year, including *Tuck Everlasting*. She had them orally "try out" their top choices for themes with partners, who commented on what they would want to read about. The teacher reminded them to try to start with a strong and interesting topic sentence. Students then shared their topic sentence drafts with a partner for comments.

GOING DEEPER: Write and Illustrate a Story for Younger Readers

Have your students interview younger students to find out what kinds of stories they like to read. Then analyze several stories for the younger grade level, and look for key features such as character development, problem, challenges, resolution, and theme. Analyze some best-selling books, and ask students why they think the book is so popular. Then ask students to use the topic ideas that they got from the interviews to write a picture book for their younger student(s). The story should have a theme that teaches them (and all readers of it) to be better people. You can brainstorm as a class various ideas for themes to develop (e.g., being a good friend, sharing, being respectful, working hard, not judging people by their looks, seeing the beauty in nature, being patient). Then have them draft the story. They can first put notes on a story map visual. Remind them to think about how the theme will be developed (e.g., Will a character start off a certain way and change because of what happens? Will a character do something unexpected to show a good quality that all people should have?).

After drafting the story and having peers help by asking clarifying questions, they storyboard it by putting parts of the text at the bottom of blank pages and sketching out the picture they will put in it. About eight to twelve pages is often enough. If possible, give them heavy paper to paint on, but they can use other media as well. It helps to give them a quick lesson on how to create engaging pictures that show key parts of the story. After writing the book, have an author's press conference to share stories, meanings, future projects, book signings, etc. Then have the authors meet with their original younger students to read the stories aloud to them.

Another variation that the younger students won't usually ask for—but can be very educational for your students—is writing a historical fiction story. You can ask the teacher of the younger students what events and people in history they are studying and then have your students choose what they want to write about.

Enhanced Shared and Collaborative Writing

In this section, I include any variation of what is often called shared or collaborative writing. The most common variation of shared writing is when the teacher leads the writing (often up on a poster or document camera) with the whole class. The teacher shares his or her questions, insights, and skills as students share what they want to communicate through the text being written together. The most common variation of collaborative writing is when groups or pairs of students write something together. Collaborative writing often follows shared writing.

Both activities build on students' existing language structures and vocabulary to help them create a product that is more advanced than what they likely could have produced without peer or teacher help. The activities tend to help students do the following:

- Better remember the content they are learning

- Identify important information to summarize

- Use complete sentences and correct punctuation

- Model language and thinking skills

- Maximize clarity by choosing the best words and grammar to use

- Learn mini lesson concepts by seeing their own words in writing

- Learn how to collaborate with others to construct a piece of academic writing

- See the thinking involved in the revising and editing process

By making authentic communication enhancements similar to the ones that follow, you can strengthen these eight advantages even more.

- Have a purpose for the shared written product that goes beyond just learning how to write in school. The purpose could be to change the minds of local government officials, a story for parents that teaches them how to parent, the next chapter of a book that they are writing throughout the year, a how-to guide, a poem for the school paper, a letter to an author, an opinion article, and so on.

- If you have an emphasis on developing a certain writing skill or using certain aspects of language, make sure students are clear on what it is, and have them explain to partners how the skill or language helps them to communicate the idea in writing to others. For example, you might have students work on, in their writing, combining two simple sentences into a complex sentence, using and punctuating dialogue, avoiding loaded language in argumentation pieces, using parallel structure, etc.

- Create prompts that help students create, choose, build up, and own the ideas that they express in their writing (e.g., "Let's write a letter from the perspective of Shiloh and how he feels at this point in the story." "Is the United States a democracy?" "Describe the water cycle from the perspective of a water molecule [or drop]." "If you could change anything going on in the world today, what would it be? Write a letter to one or more persons who could make the change happen.").

Requires and Helps Students Clarify and Support

- During the shared writing, stop and have students turn to a partner at times to ask a clarify or support question about what has been written so far. They can also write these down before they partner up. Then they share out several questions and see if the writing needs to be adjusted in some way.

- Model your zeal to use language that is as clear as possible for potential readers. And model your yearning for finding, using, and explaining the strongest evidence, data, and details as possible in order to support an idea. Say things such as "Sure, this might get me the points I want on the rubric, but I really want it to communicate the idea even better than what it's doing now. I want to change minds with my writing!"

- After the shared writing, have students pair up and read the piece aloud to each other. Then have them come up with questions that a person who is not in the class might ask about it. If it's short, students can copy the writing and take it home to share with family members, who need to ask at least two questions or offer two suggestions for improving the clarity or strength of the piece.

- Create a writing task or prompt with a reader audience that will likely want or need the information in the written product. For example, you might prompt half of your students to write an article on the pros of an issue and the other half to write on the cons. They pair up and need to read their partner's article in order to write a collaborative argument article that decides which side is stronger.

- At times during the shared or collaborative writing, stop and have students share what they think should be written next, or what words to use, or what an accompanying visual should be. They should say how the suggestion could help the clarity or strength, or communicative power of the writing.

- Have students do shared writing in small groups. They can pass the paper or computer around or have one student write down what they think is the strongest and clearest writing they can produce for a given audience. They can then share their written product with another group for feedback.

- Give students different pieces of information (pictures or short texts) that they can share during whole-class or small-group shared or collaborative writing activities.

The two versions of a shared writing activity in a fifth-grade history lesson develop writing skills by answering this question: "What were the effects of the westward expansion during the early 1800s on people and politics?" Notice how the enhanced version more effectively pushed and helped students to think and communicate like historians.

Original version. The teacher planned to start the lesson by saying something like "Even before the California Gold Rush and the railroad, people were moving west by the thousands. Why? How did life change for them? How did the nation change? How did life change for the Native Americans who had been living in these lands for thousands of years? After we read and talk about some of these answers, we will build up a historian-like idea and communicate it to others in writing. But first, we will do a shared writing in order to model some of the things that I would like for you to think about as you write your articles." Next, students would read a textbook section about the Oregon Trail and its hardships. The teacher planned to have students write a sample article together about the challenges of the Oregon Trail. He would ask them to use some of the language and skills that they covered in the shared writing activity.

Enhanced version. After the teacher asked the questions highlighted in italics in the previous paragraph, he reminded students that they are learning to think like historians. And he reminded them of five big umbrella questions that historians often ask: (1) What is important in history? (2) Why? (3) What makes history happen? (4) Did it really happen like that? (5) How did people think and feel? And he reminded them that they would get to build up a historian idea and write a short article for their school's *Young Historians Journal* that is published twice a year.

He said, "But first we will do a shared writing to learn some skills for making your articles as strong and as clear as possible so that readers of the journal can build up the new ideas in their minds from reading your articles. He had them read two articles: (1) a journal entry by a pioneer and (2) the textbook section (using some of the authentic reading ideas in Chapter 3).

He asked them if they had any ideas or questions that might help them start their shared article. One student asked, "So it looks hard. Why did they even go west if it was so hard?" Others agreed that this could be an interesting topic to write about. Here is an excerpt of the activity.

T: So how should we begin? Is there a hook we might use to get readers interested in reading it? Meet with your partner for one minute. Go. (partner talk)

A: We talked about beginning with a possible quote from a pioneer, something like: "This isn't what I expected at all. I'm not sure this is worth it."

T: What do others think? (The teacher begins to write under the document camera and read out loud.) "This isn't what I expected at all. I'm not sure this is worth it." Now how about adding to it, "How many pioneers thought this or said this as they moved west in the early 1800s?" Then what? We need to start communicating what the article will be about now.

B: What about "The trip out west was hard for a lot of reasons. But for many people it was good."

T: Okay. Is there a clearer term that we can use instead of *good?*

C: How 'bout "worth it"?

T: (after writing those two sentences) Okay. This seems like a strong enough hook and thesis statement for now, which states the main idea we are trying to build in the article. What should the next paragraph be about? Share what should we should write next with your partner. (pairs talk)

D: Maybe how it was hard? Like the diseases they got from bad water and food.

E: And the weather.

B: And running out of food.

F: And they drown in rivers.

T: Let's start with these. Okay. How do we write these? Should we just make a list? Disease, weather, food, and rivers? (multiple students: "No!") So, what do we write?

D: Explain each one.

T: Okay. I agree, but not too much because we don't want it to be too long. Our readers don't need separate paragraphs for each of the difficult aspects. Let's put them into one paragraph. (Teacher and students cowrite the paragraph.) Now, what's in our next paragraph, from our thesis?

G: The part that it was worth it for many people.

T: Okay, so how do we start it? Share with a partner. (partner talk)

C: But for many people it was worth it?

T: Okay. Let's try to avoid starting a paragraph with the word *but*. And we need to remind readers of the "it," which was the journey, right? And I want to connect to the last paragraph. So how about "Even though the journey was dangerous, many people thought it was worth the risks in the end." Does that work? Now what? Share with your partner what you think a reader will expect next. (pairs talk)

H: We think cuz it was to have their own land.

T: Okay. Do others agree? It's a solid idea, but is that all that we write?

E: No, we need to explain it and maybe share an example, like from the journal parts that we read.

(Teacher and students continue to write the shared piece. Then the teacher has them get into pairs to craft a collaboratively written response to the prompt, "But was it worth it for the Native Americans who lived in those regions?")

Notice how the teacher provided just enough language support and modeling to push students a little further in their language and writing skills, while not taking over the process. He tried to model for students the mindset of focusing on communicating to readers—not just getting points on a rubric. This writing goes up on the wall for a while for students to refer to when needed.

 ## Enhanced Use of Writing Organizers

Graphic organizers for writing have been around a long time. They include Venn diagrams; tables; flowcharts; semantic maps; T-charts; and a wide range of organizers in the shapes of flowers, buildings, plot diagrams, hamburgers, cookies, ice cream sundaes, and so on. Graphic organizers are ways to prompt for and organize information in logical, clear, and meaningful ways. The challenge, though, is to help students see that filling in graphic organizers is not just another fill-in-the-blank busywork school activity but rather a way to help them build up important ideas in the minds of the people who read their writing. We must remind students, as they visually organize and flesh out their ideas, that their ideas are valuable to the world and that writing them down for others helps to foster their sense of voice and ownership of academic ideas.

Here are some enhancements to help you make the communication in these types of activities more authentic.

Requires and Helps Students to Purposefully Build Ideas

- Make sure that there is an engaging and authentic purpose for writing and that the graphic organizer helps students achieve it. For example, if you are having students compare two characters, make sure you can explain the purpose of comparing and how the Venn diagram serves this purpose. Remind them that all writing instruction and practice is for improving how they communicate their important ideas to others.

- Use graphic organizers that help students build up ideas. Some organizers, such as tables, charts, matrices, and timelines tempt students to just list and "learn" information without placing it into a more solid and significant idea. Remind students that all writing organizers should be helpful for answering the question "What important idea are you trying to communicate, and how will you build it up in readers' minds?"

- Use an argument balance scale visual organizer for argument-based writing. (See the next Going Deeper section in this chapter.)

- Model how to use a communication mindset when filling in a prewriting graphic organizer (e.g., idea-building blueprint [see Chapter 2 or the online appendix], semantic map, outline, Venn diagram, and so on), and model how to ask clarify and support questions to improve its usefulness for writing. Model how to add more notes as a result of these questions—notes that will help the students produce much stronger first drafts. You can have students pair up and ask their partners to look at the other's filled-in organizer and ask questions about it that could help in the eventual writing.

- Create graphic organizers that have spaces (or use sticky notes) for clarifying and supporting. You can tell students that you want to see at least two clarifying and three supporting notes on the organizer. Remind students that they need to push themselves to be clearer and use more support than they tend to think is needed. If the writing will be read by many different readers (as is the case with most writing), then they need to meet the clarify and support needs of a wide range of people.

- Model how to use the filled-in graphic organizer to write sentences and paragraphs. Model how to improve the writing in response to the internal "How can I help the reader best understand this?" questions along the way. Other questions include "Does the reader already know this?" "Will the reader want me to clarify this?" "Will the reader want evidence here in order to be convinced or to build up a solid understanding of what I am trying to communicate?" "How do I highlight my most important evidence?" "How do I address the concerns and criticisms of skeptics on this issue?"

- Give two students different texts with information that they will use to cobuild a shared idea (e.g., two poems with the theme of how to be a good friend). Have students use examples from their texts to fill in one shared graphic organizer that builds up one idea.

- Have students trade graphic organizers on the same or similar topic with different partners to "permanently borrow" information from peers that they add to their own organizers and written products.

- Create, choose, and fill in a graphic organizer with the readers' needs in mind. The graphic organizer should ask for and organize information that readers of the eventual written piece will want or need (e.g., "An argumentation organizer has spaces for counter-evidences and evaluations of them."). You can even have half the class be designated readers who choose a graphic organizer that they think will best produce clear and strong writing that they will read and then give it to designated authors. These authors look at the organizer to see what information on it needs to be filled in. Then the author writes a piece for the reader.

CLASSROOM EXAMPLE: Enhancing the Use of a Writing Organizer in Fourth-Grade Science

Students needed to learn how energy converts from one form to another to produce a written report that expressed this understanding. The teacher planned to have them build windmills and think about the energy conversions that led up to the windmill turning as well as any conversions that might happen afterward (e.g., plants convert the sun's energy into chemical energy, which people eat to convert into kinetic energy, which they use to blow on the windmill blades, which converts kinetic energy into electric energy, which is then used for a wide range of things such as heating a house, lighting up a city, running machines). Notice how the features of authentic communication are better developed in the enhanced version.

Original version. Students had watched some videos and performed lab activities to learn how energy converts from one form into another. She planned to have students follow instructions for performing a lab in which they would construct windmills—some of which would be powered by fans and others by students blowing on them. They would need to then describe the various conversions that took place to power their windmills and how the energy might be converted afterward. They would fill in a visual organizer (boxes with arrows between them) for different ways in which energy was converted from one form to another. After filling in the organizer, the teacher planned to have them write up a short report that described what they had learned.

Enhanced version. The teacher told students that they needed to learn about how energy converts from one form to another because of the world's need for clean energy. She then asked them how they used energy every day. Students brainstormed answers such as burning gas on the stove to cook, using lights at night, using gasoline to power cars, using solar panels on a roof, and eating food to be able to run. She added ideas such as using food energy to make sounds and pushing a child on a swing, etc. She asked students, "Which are clean energies, and which aren't?" Students came up with wind, sun, and electricity as clean and burning gasoline in cars as not clean. The teacher then told students that a lot of electricity actually comes from burning coal, which pollutes the air.

She then introduced the energy-conversion activity that students would engage in: making a model of windmills, blowing on them, and analyzing how energy converts from one form to another. Students performed the lab and engaged in group discussions to think about how to fill in the graphic organizers focused on energy conversions. They then used the ideas from their conversations to write the introductions to feasibility reports. In the reports they needed to explain the energy conversions that they learned from their windmill labs as well as other examples that they had learned and thought about. In these introductions students needed to show their knowledge as clearly and strongly as possible in order to enhance their credibility with intended readers. Students were given time to research as many types of energy conversion as they could find, and then they were given a time to share these ideas with others before writing. As they shared what they would write, the teacher prompted listeners to ask clarifying and supporting questions.

GOING DEEPER: Argument Balance Scale

Students can use an argument balance scale graphic organizer for argumentation writing. Students can use the 2-D or 3-D version. You can make the 3-D version by cutting and folding up card stock paper into a balance bar that is wider at the bottom so it can balance on the fulcrum (a cross section would look like a triangle or trapezoid). A fulcrum could be improvised using a

Figure 6.2   Argument Balance Scale (3-D)

glue stick (pictured) or a piece of paper folded into a trapezoid. You then provide cards or sticky notes on which to record reasons, evidence, examples, and explanations using different colors for different sides. Students collaborate to generate solid reasons, evidence, and examples for each side and attach them to the cross beam. Instead of quickly jumping on one side and stating (and fighting for) an opinion, students should wait until they have built up each side. If they do lean toward a side, they should resist the temptation to withhold good information that might help to build up the other side. They co-build both sides.

To model this task, you might want to use a fishbowl conversation with a student volunteer. Emphasize that you want to talk a lot about each card. Reason-and-evidence cards should be different sizes to show the "weight" of evidence, and students should be able to explain why a card's evidence is heavy or light. Some teachers have used paper clips or stickers to represent different weights. Students get a certain number of stickers or clips that they can use on each side of the scale.

Students first write the question or issue in the center of the cross beam. They start brainstorming and putting the reasons and/or evidence on cards on one side, or they can make a list. Evidence might include data, statistics, quotations, etc. Students then work together to choose the heaviest three or four evidences for each side, putting the heaviest evidence on the largest cards. Students build up both sides and then use criteria to compare them and to choose the overall heavier one. They also should prepare to explain how they reached their decisions and made their choices.

Here is a sample piece of writing, from seventh-grade English language development (ELD), that used the balance scale to gather and organize evidence. The author, with a partner, had initially brainstormed evidence on each side. Then they chose three of the strongest pieces of evidence to go into the boxes on the scale. They didn't, as I have seen all too often, just come up with the first three most convenient pieces of evidence. Before writing, this teacher had the student explain his finalized balance scale to a partner with whom he had not worked.

SOCIAL MEDIA OR NOT?

How much time do you spend in social media? Is the time good for you or bad for you? Is it good or bad for people? First I thought it was good. I used it a lot. However, now I think that it's not helpful for us.

First of all, the good. Social media helps you connect with friends and family. They share pictures and what they do all day. Like my mom, she learns about her friends from school.

Second, it can help students do better in school. They use it to talk about homework, and it helps them. A school in Oregon made a social media program. Student grades went up 50%, and they didn't skip school so much.

Third, it can get people to vote and make a difference. Lots of people said social media got them to the 2016 presidential election. Lots said they learn how to help for disasters and problems. Like a hurricane.

Now the bad. First, lots of people get their news from it. But lots of it's false and lies. For example, 64% of people said Twitter had false news. In the Science journal it said lies spread 6 times faster than the truth on Twitter. Also, other countries use it to change how we vote in elections, like in 2016. They made up fake people and lied. That's terrible.

Second, people waste a lot of time in social media. A survey said people spend an average of 1.72 hours, but 36% say social media is the biggest waste of time in their life. Some people get a little message and read it, and then its 2 hours to get back to doing their work.

Third, 52% of students are victims of bullying online. That's over half! Middle-school children who get bullied have more chance of doing suicide.

And so I think the bad weighs more than the good. Lots of kids feel bad and try to kill themselves. People waste lots of time. They should work, or be doing homework. And the lies make people vote wrong. People don't need social media to do homework or make friends. They don't need 200 friends. These friends may post lies because they aren't real friends.

You might have your students structure the article differently, of course, but without the balance scale this writing might have been much shorter and less clear. Notice the depth and organization of this student's thinking, likely as a result of using the organizer and putting his ideas into writing. This writing was quite clear and strong, and the minor spelling and grammar issues (he had been in U.S. schools for four years) will work themselves out as long as this student keeps reading and writing for authentic reasons. It's much more important to notice the authenticity and the passion in the essay, and to consider how these can help students accelerate their learning of language, literacy, and content.

Enhanced Peer Editing, Review, and Feedback

Most of you already have your students engage in peer editing, reviewing, and giving feedback. This usually looks like students trading papers, using rubrics to put down comments in the margins or on sticky notes, and having conversations about improving the writing. The following enhancements can help students communicate more authentically, both orally and in writing, as they help each other with their written work. The enhancements also help to get students *to care more* about (a) helping the peer author write the current piece more clearly and (b) helping the peer become a better writer overall.

Requires and Helps Students to Purposefully Build Ideas

- Tell students that when they act as peer editors and reviewers, they are performing two key roles: (1) helping the author communicate an important idea to others as effectively as possible and (2) coaching the author to become a better writer overall. Emphasize how important it is for their writers to have friends who give feedback on their writing, which is a vital communication skill in life.

- As a peer editor analyzes a draft piece of writing for providing feedback, the peer fills in an idea-building blueprint (see Chapter 2 or the online appendix), sticky notes, or another organizer to keep track of how the writing is building up an idea in his or her mind. Then the peer shares this visual with the author to show the writing's strengths and needs.

- Use good and "needs-improvement" writing samples to model the type of feedback you would give to the anonymous or made-up authors of the samples. Model how to highlight what the writer did to build up an idea in your mind; the writing's strengths in doing so; and what you would like to change, add, or improve. Model the types of comments that you want students to make to one another to both value and improve writing.

Requires and Helps Students to Clarify and Support

- Collaborate with students to cocreate rubrics that highlight the importance of clarity and support in order to build up ideas in readers' minds. Elements of the rubric should focus on maximizing communication for a given audience.

- As they peer review and peer edit, have students take notes on clarity and support. Is it clear to the potential audience? Is the strongest evidence used? Is the evidence explained? If it's an argument, does it use criteria to evaluate and choose? Remind students that the more they clarify and support ideas in their writing, the more likely the ideas will stick in readers' minds or make the changes that the writing is intended to make. Remind students that their ideas are needed for helping others and improving the world, but the ideas need to be clear and well supported to do so.

- Model how to give focused feedback on clarity and support to peer authors. In a fishbowl setting, ask a student to volunteer to receive feedback on their writing. Give more positive comments than suggestions. When giving suggestions, focus on ways to more effectively help readers build the idea(s), with an extra emphasis on clarifying and supporting. You can model things such as "It really helped me build up the idea when you put this part in here because… It might help if you explain why you think this evidence is so strong. You might need to add a sentence explaining what the word *bad* means here, like what makes it bad."

Requires and Helps Students to Fill Information Gaps

- Pair students who have written about different topics, and have them trade papers to provide feedback to one another. Emphasize to students that they should try hard to learn as much new information as possible from their peer's writing and from asking them questions about it. Peer editors should make suggestions that help to fill in information gaps that the editor wants or thinks that other readers would want.

- After the peer reads the piece of writing, but before sharing comments, have the author ask the peer reviewer about what he or she learned and remembered from the piece of writing and if anything could be clearer or stronger. The author can ask questions like these: "Did it change your mind in any way?" "Did it add to your idea about…?" "What could be clearer to potential readers?" "What do you think would help it get published?"

- In groups of three, have two peers read the writing of the third student, and then have a conversation about it in front of the author, who listens and takes notes. Remind them to start with and emphasize the good parts. The two can turn to the author at times to ask any questions that emerge. At the end, the author can ask the two reviewers any questions about the writing that emerged.

- Have students put themselves in the shoes of real-life editors whose job is to maximize the readership of whatever piece of writing they are reviewing. A main focus is making sure that the writing fills in any gaps and answers any questions that large groups of potential readers might have. Use some sample writings to model how an editor might think and talk about the writing.

- Near the end of the semester or year, have students write a piece on how to write well in your class. They can use notes from their journals and put together a letter, how-to guide, website, etc., for next year's students. You can show them professional books so that they can see some of the ways in which the books organized their suggestions. You can start by saying something like "You are now accomplished authors, and others want to know your secrets."

CLASSROOM EXAMPLE: *Enhancing Peer Revision in Seventh-Grade English Language Arts*

The main focus of this lesson was to use peer revision to improve students' first drafts of their response-to-literature essays, which were focused on describing an important theme in the novel that they had just finished: *Roll of Thunder, Hear My Cry* (Taylor, 1976). In previous peer revision activities, students typically looked for spelling and punctuation errors, while occasionally posing clarify and support questions. And even though the questions were helpful, the authors rarely went back to change their writing in response to them. There are several likely reasons for this: (a) it's more work to read, think, and comment on more significant changes beyond vocabulary and grammar; (b) it's more work to make significant changes in writing, especially if it's handwritten; and (c) many students have not had enough training or practice in revising writing with a focus on communication. The enhancements in the enhanced version attempt to address these challenges.

Original version. To help improve their drafts, the teacher planned a peer reviewing activity, which students had already done several times during the year. She planned to review a checklist on the features that she wanted to see in their essays, which included the following: an engaging hook, author and title, brief summary, thesis statement, topic sentences for each paragraph, evidence, commentary, conclusion, varied sentences, correct grammar, word choice, and overall tone. Then she planned to have students trade papers. She would tell students to check for these features and ask authors questions that would help them fill any gaps in understanding.

Enhanced version. After students wrote their first drafts, the teacher emphasized the importance of asking others to provide feedback from the perspectives of real readers. She said, "Instead of just looking for spelling and punctuation issues, I want you to become like professional editors at a newspaper, magazine, or publishing company. The editor is in charge of making sure the writing is as clear and strong as possible for the intended audience. The editor gives feedback on how well the writing builds up one or more ideas in readers' minds. You can use the checklist as a guide." She put the students in pairs and continued, "Your first job right now is to have a brief discussion about this checklist. Why do you think these particular features are on the checklist? How can each of these things improve the authentic communication of an essay or similar piece of writing? What happens if they are missing?"

After asking students to share their responses with the whole group, she moved into a brief lesson on what editors do. "Now I'll model what an editor might do, and as I do so, I want you to listen for times when I ask for or give feedback on building up ideas, clarifying, and supporting with evidence. You don't have to use the idea-building blueprint visual, but it might help. You can take notes on it to discuss with the author afterward. When you do provide feedback, make sure to start and end with positive comments that are genuine and connected to the writing. Feel free to get especially excited about new insights and ideas that you haven't seen or discussed in class before. And authors, you don't just sit there and agree. I want you to ask how different parts of the writing communicated to your peer reviser."

Here is a sample discussion on the topic in which the partners offered each other feedback to validate and improve the writing.

A: I really liked your idea of how greed…greediness can cause racism. That's what you were building up, right?

B: Sort of. I didn't say exactly it *caused* racism but makes it worse.

A: Okay, so maybe make that clear in your first paragraph, like even in the first sentence.

B: Okay.

A: And you started right off with examples of racist and greedy people, like Granger and Wallace. That's good. But I think it might also help somewhere in the beginning or end to describe how Mama was teaching about the money people made from slavery.

B: Yeah. That might tell readers it's not just in this story. It's bigger.

A: And I think some direct quotes could help when you talk about Granger and Wallace. Like when you say they make money from being racists. Someone reading it may want to know how.

(*Continued*)

(Continued)

B: Okay.

A: Also, I wonder, why you think Granger wants the Logan land so much? I don't think just to get his land back.

B: I don't either. I think he hates them so much he wants to take everything from them.

A: But why? Where's his hate come from?

B: Maybe cuz they're black, and he didn't think black people should own land. I can put some of that in the intro and in the paragraph on Granger. (silence) So, did you get anything new out of reading my writing?

A: Yeah, my theme was on injustice and Cassie learning how things aren't fair. Your idea about greed adds to mine, and I think even makes it stronger. Like why aren't things fair? Now, I think a lot of it comes from greed.

B: And being stupid.

A: Yeah.

This conversation has a lot of great suggestions and helpful insights that the students develop together—all of which serve to improve the communication power of the writing for both of them. In fact, even the last part about being stupid might yield some interesting insights, and extra writing, if elaborated upon. Also notice the focus on building ideas, clarifying, and improving the evidential support.

CLASSROOM EXAMPLE: Enhancing Peer Reviews in Ninth-Grade Algebra

Writing in math offers students a chance to work out their thinking, and peer reviews of mathematical writing can amplify this good thinking as students work together to clarify and support important mathematical ideas for others in written form. For this reason, I added this example focused on math. In both versions of this lesson, students are writing down their learning and are being asked to comment on the quality of their classmates' writing.

Original version. The teacher planned to start by having a student read out loud the standard for the week that was posted up on the wall: "Students will be able to solve problems and describe linear relationships between quantities by using equations and analyzing graphs." Next, the teacher would put up a video of a large mining pump that was pumping water out of a huge square pit. She would ask, "What questions come to your mind as you watch this?" Then she would ask students to share many different questions, such as "How many gallons per second does that thing pump? How long will it take to drain the pit?" After discussing the various questions and problems that result from them, she would give students a specific problem, including the quantities needed to solve it, then circulate to help them and observe their strategies. She planned to ask several students to share their solutions with the whole class, pointing out how several solutions can produce the right answers. Then she would model how to solve several other problems related to the standard. At the end of the lesson, she planned to tell students to write down a paragraph that explained how to solve problems with linear relationships.

Enhanced version. The teacher started by asking, "So, why do we practice solving problems in math?" They answered, "Because that's what you do in math. To get a good grade on tests. To be good at business and using money." She said, "Yes, I do want you to be able to solve problems, but I really want you to understand how math works. That's why we solve math problems. And knowing how math works helps you in a lot of jobs, sciences, engineering, and so on. So whenever you solve a math problem, I want you to be thinking about how math works, asking questions, and building up ideas. I also want you to be able to clearly describe your idea in writing, which I will ask you to do at the end of the class period today. And I will have you peer review one another's writing to help you communicate better when you write about math. I suggest that you fill in and use the math idea-building blueprint (in Chapter 2 or the online appendix). You can use it to write to future students in this class in order to help them understand linear relationships and graphing. I will pick several to read to them next year. We will begin by watching a short video of a mining pump. As you watch, think about how it shows or relates to our learning, and also think about a problem you could write about the video." After watching the video, the teacher continued, "Now meet with partners to come up with a problem about linear relationships or graphing, and then discuss how it supports your math understandings. I will come around to help and make suggestions. Then you will trade problems, solve them, and take notes about linear relationships on your blueprints."

After the trading and solving, the teacher modeled the solving of two other problems and gave the students time to work through two additional problems on their own. Then she had them to write up their explanations of the important math ideas that could be shared with future students. She reminded students to use their notes and problems that they had put on their blueprint organizers, suggesting ways to begin: "You might start with 'Have you ever watched…?' or 'In life it is important to understand linear relationships because…' Remember to be as clear and strong with your examples as possible." When students had finished writing, she had them work in groups of three: "Now trade papers and give one another feedback on how clear and strong the writing is. Clear means using the best language possible for readers—even if you have to write extra sentences. And strong means using mathematical principles and sample problems to support the idea. So readers, when you give feedback, focus on how clear and strong the idea is, as well as how effectively you think next year's students will learn from reading it."

Here is an example of Student D's first draft of her written idea, followed by a feedback conversation with Student C, followed by Student D's second draft based on the feedback. Notice how the conversation influenced and improved the clarity, strength, and length of Student D's second draft.

Student D's First Draft

My idea is that we can solve problems and show relationships between numbers by using equations and analyzing graphs. In problems you need to draw it first and then maybe draw a table and a graph for the table. Then where the lines cross it's the answer. Or you figure out the equation and solve it by moving numbers to one side and the variable on the other.

Feedback Conversation

C: This is a great start! I like how you describe how to solve the main problems that we have had. But I think it would be good to have more specific examples to support your idea. Like remember the video with the pump? And—

D: And maybe the one about the money?

C: Yeah. But you can't just write them and say how to solve them. You need to write how they are examples of the big idea.

D: I don't even know what it means. I copied it.

C: You do, I think, like when you mention the table and graph and equations. Those are all ways to show linear relationships. Like the water. It's a constant rate. If the rate changes, then it doesn't work.

D: Because it wouldn't be a line, right?

C: Yeah. So, oh, and don't forget those car and train problems. You wrote one, right?

D: Yeah. About a bike and a car.

C: Use that too. And you should mention how *x* and *y* relate on the graph and the table. I think that would help readers.

Student D's Revised Writing After Talking to Student C

My idea is that we can show and predict situations using graphs and equations with variables in them. For lines, the input is the *x* on the graph, and the *y* is the output. And all the points end up on the same line. For example, the big water pump. It goes out at a constant rate. You could try looking at the graph, but it's too big a number so I just used the equation $y = 10x$. And I solved to find *x*. Another example is if you save the same amount of money each week, you can graph it and predict what you have after any number of weeks in the future. That would be solving for *y*. And you can also predict when something will catch something else. Like the problems when a faster car or a train tries to catch a slower one that left sooner. We used the formula for distance: speed times time. Then we set the equations equal to each other and got the time they meet. In the car and bike problem, I did this with a table, graph, and equation, and all of their answers were 12 minutes.

GOING DEEPER: Using Rubrics to Guide Written Communication

Rubrics are mentioned in some of the enhancements in this chapter, but I wanted to include several more suggestions for using them here:

- Make sure students know that the rubric is meant to help them communicate better through writing. Writings may still be scored, but getting the points needs to be less important than communicating well.

- In collaboration with your students, create a rubric that focuses on clearly and strongly communicating to readers. Creating rubrics with students allows them more ownership of the process, plus a better understanding of the elements of the rubric.

- Analyze other writing samples using the draft rubric. Analyze writing for how well it communicates. It is vital for students to see other examples of writing—both good and bad—in order to identify which techniques to emulate in their own writing and to recognize flaws that undermine clarity. Finding the right samples to analyze isn't always easy. Most schools and districts have writing samples for each grade level that you can use. You can also do an Internet search for sample essays, benchmark writing samples, model essays, etc. Or use and modify student writing from previous assignments.

- Have students work together to "coassess" sample pieces by using the rubric or checklist that the teacher will eventually use to assess the writing. This helps students develop habits of self- and peer assessing their own writing during—rather than after—the writing process.

SUMMARY

Writing is a little like hiking to the top of a mountain with a heavy pack. It's hard work, you have a destination in mind, and you don't have much time or energy to take a lot of extraneous detours. Writing takes lots of practice, perseverance, patience, observation, guidance from more proficient experts (e.g., you), and feedback from peers. You need to know what it means to communicate in writing in a given grade level and discipline. You must know the ins and outs of the craft well enough to clearly explain and model them to your students. Then you must clearly communicate to students what is expected in their writing. And the more you can enhance typical writing instruction with features of authentic communication, the more engaged your students will be and the more they will want to go beyond the bare minimum to communicate their many brilliant ideas in writing.

REFLECTION QUESTIONS

1. Right now, what do your students consider to be the main purpose of writing?

2. How do experts in the discipline(s) that you teach use writing to communicate?

3. Think of a common activity that either intentionally develops writing or depends a lot on writing (e.g., writing up a lab report, creating a museum exhibit, writing an argumentation article). How authentic is it? How strong are the three features of authentic communication? How might it be enhanced?

4. What do you see as the biggest challenge in getting your students to engage in writing to communicate versus writing for points and grades?

AUTHENTIC CONVERSING

A conversation has a spirit of its own…
That is, it allows something to "emerge" which hence forth
exists.

—Hans-Georg Gadamer

Classroom conversation is an educational gold mine that still needs a hefty amount of exploration. In recent decades, millions of students in many settings have missed out on chances to learn by conversing with others. As a result, these students have missed out on the many benefits, described in the next section, that come from having high-quality conversations with others in school. Yes, it's a strong claim, but think about the many students who disengaged from classroom learning because they didn't have a chance to process, clarify, strengthen, build, and voice their ideas with others in conversation.

Effective conversations are more than just listening plus speaking. Students need to know how to connect with the thoughts and feelings of the other person and to work with others to robustly build up one or more ideas. They need to know how to listen well while thinking about what to say next, and they must know when and how to use conversation skills to build and evaluate ideas.

One of the major challenges in improving classroom conversations is that student-student conversation hasn't seemed to fit into the traditional views of teaching, learning, and assessing. Conversation doesn't seem to support the many machine-scored, test-driven approaches of the past several decades. And it does take a fair amount of work to weave conversations and their skills into lessons. They do take time, and they are often loud and messy. You don't know what the majority of your students are saying all the time, and conversations are hard to assess. (Are you convinced yet?)

One of the advantages of back-and-forth conversations is that they have more ingrained potential for authentic communication than many of the more one-way school tasks have. Often when you get two or more people talking and listening to each other, they tend to want to work together to build up an idea or two, especially if they know how to use conversation skills. Partners who expect you to talk and listen to them will often push you to think and talk more than if you just sat there learning on your own. Students in a good conversation usually need to clarify and support their ideas, and they usually share different enough ideas to have information gaps.

Conversations are powerful ways to develop a variety of productive skills, content, and language in our students. Here are some of the benefits of talk in the classroom that many of this chapter's enhancements tend to cultivate. Conversations help students to do the following:

- *Develop more robust content understandings.* As they talk with others, students often realize that they aren't clear on certain concepts (e.g., when a peer says "Huh?" or gives a quizzical look). Often, peers can explain ideas better than the teacher or textbook can. And every time students share and negotiate ideas with peers, their brains work to shape and clarify their evolving knowledge and skills.

- *Learn more about the richness of human diversity.* Students get to learn a variety of other perspectives, values, knowledges, motivations, fears, goals, interests, likes, dislikes, cultures, ways of communicating, etc.

- *Increase their agency and ownership of learning.* Most students appreciate the freedom to build and shape ideas with others—not just memorize things for tests or follow a script written by someone else. They tend to learn more by creating, teaching, and explaining to each other—and sometimes challenging one another. Conversation often gets students' brains into higher gear because, as they try to synthesize, organize, and clarify thoughts for real others in real time, they make ideas clearer for themselves.

- *Use language in different ways.* Students gain real practice using new vocabulary in context, and they hear a wide range of grammatical structures from different conversation partners. Students get a chance to try out emerging ideas on others in safe settings, get them validated or modified, and practice describing them before talking to larger groups. With every other turn in a paired conversation, students listen to input and produce oral output, which are two vital dimensions of language learning.

- *Build their academic listening skills.* While even nonacademic listening skills need work, it's even harder to develop academic listening, which entails listening to a partner's every turn and processing the information in ways that build up or challenge academic ideas. It means remembering the key points, recognizing inconsistencies, evaluating evidence, and so on. Conversations provide lots of practice for improving this type of listening.

- *Build their reading skills.* Conversations with others can help students understand complex texts by developing skills such as summarizing, making inferences, asking questions, supporting ideas with evidence, etc. Think about the power of having students describe these skills to one another and talk about their understandings of content in conversations before, during, and after reading texts year after year.

- *Build their writing skills.* Conversations tend to clarify ideas and allow students to get evidence from others that can help writers to flesh out and build up key ideas in their written compositions.

- *Develop "inner conversation" skills while reading, writing, and learning.* Conversations play a big role in shaping the inner talk that fills our minds all day. Conversations with others shape the language, ideas, and values that we use to think about what we learn and how we live.

Consider why the three features are so important in conversation. For example, if students don't build up at least one idea in a conversation, they are more likely to get sidetracked or off task. If clarifying and supporting are not needed, scaffolded, or encouraged by one another or by you, then the conversation will likely be short and shallow. And if one student already has all the information needed to build up an idea and to accomplish a task, then the student doesn't need to converse with a partner. We want to set up conversation situations in which students feel that they will do much better building up ideas if they converse and collaborate with others.

CORE CONVERSATION SKILLS

There are many skills needed to engage in productive conversations, but in classrooms I tend to have students focus on developing five skills. You are already familiar with the first four, as they stem from two of the three features of authentic communication.

Building up one or more ideas. In a conversation, this skill acts like a project manager, guiding students' conversational decisions as they work to keep the focus on building ideas. Students using this skill proficiently have thoughts such as "I don't think we have strong enough evidence for this idea. Let's keep looking." "I don't think this is a relevant enough idea to build, looking at the prompt." "We have used this word a lot, and it's not helping us anymore." "We need to better understand our criteria for comparing the two sides of this argument." "I think we need to build up this idea even more." This is more of a meta skill, one that requires zooming out at times as well as zooming in on key parts to explore and develop: "What does … mean? A question that comes up here is … Your point about… reminds me of the fact that… Let's zoom out a bit to think about what we need at this point." This skill helps students decide which other skills are needed at certain points in the conversation in order to most effectively build up ideas.

Posing a relevant and buildable idea. This skill requires students to come up with an idea that can be built up in conversation. It should be an idea that responds to the prompt and helps students to learn what they are supposed to learn in the lesson. Even though this might seem like a skill that we cannot develop in students, we can. This chapter offers several ideas that will help students to generate good ideas and decide which ones have the most potential for building up in conversation.

Clarifying. A great many of the words and sentences that we use don't mean the exact same thing in the mind of another person. This is especially true when students are building up complex and academic ideas. As a result, they need to push peers and selves for clarity considerably more often than they think they need to. They can do this by asking questions ("What do you mean by…?" "How…?" "Why…?" "Who…?" "What…?" "Where…?"); paraphrasing to confirm their own understandings ("So you are saying that…"); actively reading the other person's face for signs of confusion; and using a wide range of gestures, expressions, prosody, and even visuals. The ability to clarify results in a shared understanding allows students to be on the same page when it comes to what things mean. But this shared understanding is a challenge.

In the last paragraph, I used the phrase "more often than they think they need to." I want to emphasize this because the more we can get students to do more clarifying (and supporting) than they think is needed, the more prepared they are for the real world, and the more their ideas get built up and stick in their minds. The downside, as always, is that this work takes time and energy. In a pair-share, for example, how many students, on their own accord, ask their partners to clarify something? In their minds, it means that they both need to work more to listen and speak. We should therefore train students to not accept one-word, short, abstract, or minimal responses and instead to ask for more. Not only will this help clarify meanings and extend the conversation, but it will also show the talker that the listener is interested. At the same time, we must train students, as they speak, to feel uncomfortable when they have said too little or see confusing looks on partner faces.

Supporting. Teachers have been telling students to "support your ideas" for a long time, but students have often done so out of obligation or for points, especially when asked to do so in writing. As this book has argued many times already, we must transform students' mindsets more into thinking, "I need to strengthen each idea as much as possible by using the best evidence and reasoning possible." This mindset change cannot be achieved by a bookmark or a simple poster on the wall reminding students to ask for evidence. Instead, we need to engage students in authentic conversations and activities in which they need and want to learn how to support ideas as effectively as possible. We want them to think, as they converse, that they *need* to support their ideas well, and that if they don't, it matters.

Evaluating and choosing. When there are two or more competing ideas (e.g., an argument), students need to evaluate the "weight" of the evidence supporting both sides of the issue or decision and then choose which one weighs more. This skill is often used when reading controversial texts, watching the news, or just making tough decisions.

When there is a need to choose between two or more ideas in a conversation, I suggest using a process called collaborative argumentation. To collaboratively argue, students work together to build up both sides and then collaborate to evaluate and choose a side. They should use criteria to evaluate the value or weight of the evidence on each side, but because people tend to differ in their values, they can end up disagreeing on which side weighs more. This is okay, as long as students work to clarify their values, perspectives, and criteria being used.

Collaborative argumentation is very different from the common types of argumentation and persuasion that students tend to see in the media, at home, and among friends. Students often see and participate in *competitive* argumentation, where their thinking is focused on winning. This occurs when a person quickly picks one side and avoids considering or building up the evidence of the opposing side. This usually stems from the person being biased, uninformed, and/or politically or selfishly motivated. Truth and good decision-making (and civilization) tend to erode when this happens, and we want our students to be better at thinking and deciding than what we are currently seeing out in the world.

Hand Motions for Prompting and Remembering the Skills

I encourage teachers to teach hand motions like these so that (a) teachers can prompt students to use more of these skills without interrupting their conversations; (b) students can remind each other to use different skills by using the motions in conversation; and (c) students can remember, kinesthetically, the skills with so much going on in a real-time conversation.

- *Building up an idea*: Stack hands up on one another toward the ceiling.

- *Posing a relevant idea*: Lay one hand out in front of you with the palm up.

- *Clarifying*: Cover face with thumbs and index fingers touching, palms out, then spread hands and fingers apart.

- *Supporting ideas*: Lay one hand down out front with palm down. Bring the other hand up underneath with five fingers facing up to support the palm-down hand.

- *Evaluating and choosing*: Put both arms out to each side, palms up, and move them up and down like a seesaw or balance scale.

For over a decade, I have been recording and analyzing conversation samples and researching their effects on student learning. One of the most interesting findings was that conversations in which students used more than three clarifying moves, and more than two supporting moves per idea were considered by their teachers as having a high potential for learning. A prompt for clarification or support and its response were counted as one move. I also found that when there was one or fewer clarifying moves and one or fewer supporting moves per idea, teachers deemed the conversations to have minimal potential. Some conversations were long but had minimal potential because they had multiple ideas that lacked multiple clarifications and supports for each one. These were what I call "popcorn" conversations in which there were lots of ideas popping up but little development of any one of them. This means that we can't just have students use a lot of skills (and sentence frames for the skills) and expect effective conversations. They need to use the skills to focus on and build up meaningful ideas.

These five skills don't just develop on their own. They don't come naturally to many students, and they aren't easy to develop and practice. So it's important to (a) stress their value for learning and for life and (b) provide engaging and motivating reasons to use the skills in conversations. Thus, one of the purposes of the enhancements in this chapter is to show students how working together to construct ideas is worth it in the short run, the long run, and the intermediate run.

Two Vital Practices for Productive Conversations

I. *Valuing others' ideas.* One of the most important (yet least assessed) results of having students converse in class is the feeling that others value their ideas. This leads to other important feelings of agency, ownership, and confidence. Students can improve in their abilities to value the ideas of others by doing the following:

- Helping a partner build up an idea by spending time on it, saying that you like the idea, and not quickly shoving a partner's ideas aside to switch to one's own idea

- Backchanneling, which is when you say things like Wow! Really? No way! Uh-huh. Seriously? Great point! Interesting. Hmm

- Focused listening, which includes an attentive posture, head nodding, and appropriate eye contact

- Paraphrasing and asking questions that show you want to know more about what the person is saying

(Continued)

(Continued)

2. *Using nonverbal cues and prosody.* As you know, nonverbal cues carry a lot of the communication load when conversing with others. Nonverbal cues include using gestures, body movements, head nods, facial expressions (smiles, looks of concern, surprise, excitement, pensiveness), and silence. And many students who spend a lot of time on screens lack practice in (a) seeing good models of nonverbal communication and (b) using nonverbal cues to communicate their ideas. Prosody keeps one from sounding robotic—it is what you do with the language to emphasize thoughts, such as rising or falling pitch in words and sentences, stressing words and syllables with more or less loudness, lengthening or shortening words and phrases, and pausing. Often these prosodic features are coupled with facial expressions and gestures to improve and clarify speaking every other turn.

AUTHENTIC CLASSROOM CONVERSATIONS

Here are several examples of common conversation activities and how they can be enhanced to make them more authentic, instructional, and meaningful.

 ### Enhanced Whole-Class Discussions

Whole-class discussions, used in most classrooms, offer a unique opportunity to regularly model and practice meaningful conversations with students. Doing so can mean changing familiar patterns such as long teacher presentations with sporadic student input or brainstorm-popcorn sessions in which students share a wide range of thoughts and ideas but don't build up ideas in significant ways. The enhancements that follow were chosen and designed to help all students in the classroom learn from whole-class conversations in which they use the core skills to build up academically valuable ideas in their minds.

Requires and Helps Students to Purposefully Build Ideas

- Focus the discussion explicitly on building up or choosing a particular idea. Make sure students know what this idea is at one or more points before, during, or after the discussion. For example, in an argument-based discussion, tell the class that they will use the discussion time to first build up the pro side of the issue, then the con side, and then they will collaboratively evaluate which side is more strongly supported by evidence.

- Display a large visual organizer such as a semantic map, an idea-building blueprint (see Chapter 2 or the online appendix), or an argument balance scale (see Chapter 6) where you (or a student scribe) take notes on the details, evidence, and reasons that come up in the discussion. Students can take notes on smaller versions of this visual and add to them during the discussion and beyond.

- Stop halfway through the discussion to have students reflect on what they all still need to talk about to accomplish the purpose of the discussion (e.g., "We need to clarify the term *assimilation*." "We need to come up with better evidence for the con side of the argument."). They can quickly meet in pairs to come up with and try out some initial suggestions.

Requires and Helps Students to Clarify and Support

- After you or a student shares a potentially useful thought or opinion, unless it was complete and perfectly clear to all, students should ask questions that require the speaker to think of ways to clarify or support what they said. You can give a visual cue or hold up a card for times in which you really want one type of question. I have also seen teachers prompt for this simply by being silent. When the teacher doesn't talk, it's a cue for students to step in.

- As you plan the whole-class discussion, think about how to maximize the number of students who participate in discussions overall, without depending on cold-calling or on the same five students who tend to volunteer to share. This might include allowing students to take breaks to write down ideas and practice in either pairs or to themselves what they might say. It includes listening in on pair-shares and, after hearing a good idea from a reticent speaker, asking the student if she or he would share the idea with the entire class.

- You or students can use colored cards or signals such as one finger for something urgent and relevant right now, two fingers for a clarifying response or question, three fingers for a support response or question, and four fingers for a new or opposing topic to build up.

Requires and Helps Students to Fill Information Gaps

- Give students different texts, pictures, or cards with information on them that they can share with the class during discussion. If they have the same text, they can meet beforehand to brainstorm any information or insights they might want to share when the whole-class discussion starts.

- Stop the whole-class discussion at times to have students pair up and respond to a question just posed by a student. Tell them that they will need to share a synopsis of what their partners share with them; you circulate around the room to listen for ideas that you can use to further the discussion.

- Ask questions to fill genuine information gaps that *you* have—that is, questions that students know that you don't know the answers to. These questions can ask for opinions, perspectives, personal experiences, information from texts that they have read and you haven't, etc.

CLASSROOM EXAMPLE: *Enhancing Whole-Class Discussion in Sixth-Grade History*

In both versions of the lesson, students are learning about the contributions of Ancient Greece to modern ideas of democracy and citizenship. Notice how the enhanced version establishes a more engaging purpose for the research and for the whole-class discussion.

Original version. The teacher planned to have students first read and take notes on a section of the textbook on the early forms of democracy. The teacher would start by telling students that the lesson will focus on how democracy got its start in Ancient Greece and what it meant to be a citizen back then. The teacher would start the discussion by outlining the types of government that Athens had up until Solon, Cleisthenes, and Pericles introduced democratic ideas and changes in the system of government. Then he would ask, "So what changes did they make, and how were they democratic?" The teacher would guide the discussion to help students improve their answers and to prompt them to add certain ideas and definitions to their notes.

Enhanced version. The day before, students had done an activity that helped them learn several terms, such as *oligarchy, tyranny, monarchy, democracy,* and *citizen.* The teacher started this lesson by telling students, "Ancient Athens is often called the birthplace of democracy. But what is democracy? Pair up to compare it to other forms of government. Use what you learned from yesterday's activity to briefly share your definition or add to your partner's definition." Students then shared basic definitions and comparisons. The teacher said, "So now let's see what happened in Athens, and if you think it really was the birth of democracy." Different groups of students then read one of three different short texts on the birth of democracy, one of which was the textbook section. When they had finished reading, the teacher started the discussion this way: "Okay, so we need to build up two sides, right? The yes and the no sides. We can make an argument scale visual as we discuss. What should we start with? The yes side? Okay, first, share with a partner some reasons for yes, it was the beginning of democracy. (Several minutes pass.) Now share with the whole class."

Here is a portion of the whole-class discussion focused on this question: Was Ancient Athens the birthplace of democracy? Note: The letters *A* through *J* represent the students; the letter *T* is the teacher.

A: One good reason for yes was more people got to make decisions, not just the oligarchy people.

T: Any clarifying questions?

B: What's oligarchy?

A: When like small groups of rich people, or families, control the government.

C: Yeah, Cleisthenes split up people in groups by where they lived, not by being rich, and some people were chosen for the Council of 500 by, it says by lot.

D: Like a lottery, right?

T: Yes, okay. But are we done? What could we ask now?

E: Um, anything more we can say to build up the yes side?

F: I think the quote by Pericles should be up there: "Its administration favors the many instead of the few; this is why it is called a democracy…class considerations not being allowed to interfere with merit; nor again does poverty bar the way, if a man is able to serve the state, he is not hindered by the obscurity of his condition" (Thucydides, circa 430 BCE). (silence)

T: Okay, a lot in there. How can we respond to that so that we keep building up our idea?

D: Ask what it means?

G: I think it means you can be poor and still make decisions, like be a part of government. That's democracy, because there's no king or dictator.

T: Okay, let's write these things down on the yes side of the scale here. (writes) So if we think we have built up the yes side enough, how about the no side?

H: Well, only men who owned property and were born in Athens were citizens. So the women and slaves couldn't do any politics. So if democracy is rule by all people, then that wasn't democracy.

I: Yeah, you might even call it just a bigger oligarchy.

(Continued)

(Continued)

B: What?

I: Well, so you have more people, those men, but it's still a group, and a lot of others can't join that group, so, oligarchy, I think.

J: I also think it wasn't good that they kicked people out of the country if they wanted to be powerful. That doesn't seem like democracy.

E: Why not?

J: Um, because…

T: Wait. I would like everyone to take a moment to think about why or why not banishing a person from the country is democratic.

The discussion continued, and the teacher had students, in pairs, decide which side weighed more. The class decided that it wasn't a great example of democracy but that it qualified enough to be called the birthplace, especially when considering the quotation by Pericles. Notice how little the teacher talked and how the teacher tried to push facilitation moves out to students rather than be the hub and controller of all turns. Notice, too, the engaging purpose for discussing, the pushing for clarifying and supporting, and the information gaps that resulted from having students read different texts and share their differing opinions and reasons. FYI, the follow-up discussion the next day was prompted by "So after democracy was 'born,' why didn't other governments immediately adopt it? Why do you think other forms of government still dominated for thousands of years?"

 Enhanced Small-Group Conversations

In a small group conversation, like any other conversation, the main goal should be to work together to cobuild one or more ideas as robustly as possible in every goup member's mind. This means that students must listen to one another; push one another to clarify and add support to ideas; and, when there is an argument, work together to build up both sides and decide which has the strongest evidence. When students do these things, small group conversations tend to work well and be worth the time.

The problem is that, with all the variables involved (student differences, interests, knowledge, engagement, etc.), many small-group conversations are not as effective as they could be. The most common problem is that one or two students dominate the talk while the other students just listen or lose focus. And a related problem is that talkative students sometimes don't listen to the ideas of other group members even when they do share. Another problem is that the prompts and purposes are not engaging enough to motivate and guide students to build up ideas together. And a challenge already mentioned in other chapters is that many students still need to develop the mindset of pushing themselves to use the best evidence and clearest language to build up important ideas as well as possible. The following enhancements attempt to address these problems and challenges.

Requires and Helps Students to Purposefully Build Ideas

- Have a purpose for the small-group conversation that goes beyond just taking notes, filling in a graphic organizer, or making a poster. Have them make a decision, build up an argument, create something new, solve a problem, or create a useful or interesting product. Remember that conversing takes a lot of energy, and it needs to be worth it.

- When discussing the meaning of a text, create prompts that help students (1) understand the text as a whole, (2) build up key ideas intended by the author, and/or (3) learn more about how and why authors write in certain ways. Then have students pause at times during the conversation to make sure they are building up the response to the prompt. Or if it deviates a bit, they can check with you to see if what they are talking about is productive enough to continue.

- Don't always give specific roles to students. Have them all cofacilitate, all take notes, all share evidence, etc. If you do have roles, try adding the role of idea builder, someone who makes sure all that they are talking about is useful for building the focal idea(s). This person might also fill in an organizer like the idea-building blueprint (see Chapter 2 or the online appendix) or use other note-taking strategies, like taking quick notes on different colored note cards and stacking them up to show how different clarifying and supporting moves are used by members to build up an idea.

Requires and Helps Students to Clarify and Support

- Do a fishbowl with several student volunteers to model group participation and idea-building skills, such as deciding on the most relevant ideas to build, asking for clarification, pushing for higher-quality support, valuing others' contributions, using nonverbal cues, evaluating evidence, etc.

Stop the conversation at times to ask the observers (a) what skill they just saw being used and how it was helpful to the conversation and (b) what would be the next thing to say to keep building the idea and accomplish the purpose of the conversation.

- During the small-group conversation, as they are listening, encourage students to write down short clarifying or supporting question notes that will enhance their understanding of the speaker's idea or help the speaker to expand and deepen it. These can be written on a visual organizer or on small cards or sticky notes. Examples include one or two words with a question mark after them: Why fight? How? Evidence? Freedom? Short-term v. long? This helps students not to forget that they have a question while not cutting off the current speaker's sharing and not looking down too long to write a full question. If the notes are on an idea-building organizer, students can see how these notes and questions build up the idea(s).

- If you notice that students need to solidify their learning of a handful of key terms, put the terms on cards and put the cards into envelopes. Then challenge small groups to come up with meaningful ways to organize them, such as in categories, a sequence, a web of relationships, sentences on a picture, etc. Remind them to push each other for clarification of the terms and to provide a rationale for why they are organized in a certain way.

Requires and Helps Students to Fill Information Gaps

- For discussing literature, ask group members to focus on and explore different topics within the same work of literature, such as symbols, dialogues, character motivations, key events, themes, figurative language, etc. Then have them come together and share their insights based on their focal topic. Have them weave together the different topics into a final idea or argument (e.g., "The author of *Holes* [Sachar, 1998] effectively used key literature techniques to tell an interesting and meaningful story. First, …"). Students can also focus on the same literary topic, read different works, and come together to discuss them (e.g., "A very important literary device that authors use to show rather than tell is figurative language. For example, in ….").

- For nonfiction, ask group members to first read (or watch or listen to) the text and take notes with a focus on different topics, writing techniques, or sections. Then they share their focus in the group conversation in order to build up their larger idea(s). For example, a teacher might tell Student A to focus on researching the background of the author of the primary source, B to focus on loaded and biased language in the text, C to focus on the main idea(s) of the source, D to focus on causes and effects described in the source, and E to focus on understanding the thoughts and feelings of the people in that time period described by the source.

- Use prompts that require students to use their varying knowledges, backgrounds, values, and opinions. Most students have plenty of opinions. For example, ask students to share their opinions in order to jointly make decisions on social, ethical, or political issues. In science, they can share observations they have done outside of class or data from labs they did inside of class.

- In math, give students different problems to solve, and then share in the group so that the group can build up an idea of how math works based on what each of their problems is showing and supporting.

- Spend extra time and energy on making sure that the typically reticent students want to and have a chance to share in the small groups. You can have students use strategies such as sharing chips or cards that are put into the middle, stopping to allow students who haven't said much in the past three minutes to share, or passing around an object or visual organizer to write on and share from. (They can use different colored pens to write with.) Remind all students that half of the purpose of the small-group conversation is to practice listening and speaking to others. Also remind students to be highly respectful and inclusive of different students' ideas.

CLASSROOM EXAMPLE: Enhancing Small Group Discussion in Third-Grade English Language Arts

Students were starting a unit on short stories, and the day's lesson in both versions was focused on inferring character traits from their words and actions. Notice the differences between the two versions, particularly with respect to the purpose and modeling.

Original version. After an introduction to stories and their key parts the day before, the teacher planned to start off the lesson by reading a story aloud. She would pause her reading at times to think aloud, pointing to specific actions and words and how they suggest certain character traits. After a few such pauses, she would ask the class for help with one more. Then she would tell students to get into their reading groups, read a different story, and discuss their inferences about a character. For example, students in the blue reading group would be given *The Empty Pot* (Demi, 1996), a Chinese folktale about a boy who tries and fails to grow a cooked seed given to him by the emperor, who eventually chooses the boy to be his successor because of his honesty.

Enhanced version. The teacher started the lesson by saying, "As you know, we are working on creating a list of recommended stories for third graders for next year. We are looking for stories that have interesting characters and good life lessons. Today we will be reading and evaluating the *The Empty Pot* for themes that will help third graders and others who read it become better people. Authors don't usually say a theme directly. We have to pay special attention to clues that they offer. Today we are looking for clues in the characters' words and actions. I will use a fishbowl activity to model an example from one story that we read yesterday, 'The Crystal Ball'." She and three student volunteers formed a group in the middle of the room, and they had a conversation about the story, focusing on character actions and words. As students brought up character actions, words, and inferences about them, the teacher wrote notes on large sticky notes and put them up on a flip chart version of the idea-building blueprint without the idea at the top filled in. She then asked, "So now, what theme should we put up top? What are these inferences supporting?" They came up with this idea: "It's important to be happy with what you have." Then as a group they agreed to remove several sticky notes that didn't support that theme.

After this modeling, she read *The Empty Pot* aloud and had students fill in small sticky notes on character words and actions that they thought might build up one or more themes. Then she said, "Student A in each of your small groups will help to make sure that you all are building up your theme idea from *The Empty Pot* and using story actions and words to do so. Student B, you will fill in the idea-building blueprint for the group. And when any group member shares, especially if it's a short share or thin on information, others should ask a clarify or support question to help with the idea building. Once you have decided on a key theme, each one of you should think of a personal application of that theme to share with another person in the room who was not in your group."

Here is an excerpt from a small-group conversation during the lesson.

C: I think the theme is to be honest.

B: Why?

C: He was the only kid who brought an empty pot.

A: But how is that honest?

C: The other kids lied.

B: But they didn't say anything.

C: But they brought their pots with plants to the king. And the king told them to grow the seed he gave them. So they put other seeds in it, but the king seed was bad so nothing would grow.

A: Why'd he do that?

B: I don't think he cared about how big it, it was to test them, like, if they'd lie.

D: And they did.

B: Yeah. So what do I put down?

A: To be honest and not lie, because then maybe you get to be king.

D: We're not gonna be kings.

B: No, but bad things happen to people who lie.

A: Like what?

D: They go to jail, maybe. And when I lie to my mom, I get in big trouble.

C: But so it's good to be honest.

This conversation has short turns, but it is not dominated by any one student, and they do a nice job building up the idea of the value of being honest. They use evidence from the book and stay on topic throughout, prompting for clarification and support. Small-group discussions like this one can be of great benefit to students, especially when they have the mindset of and the skills for co-constructing ideas.

Enhanced Paired Conversations

Paired conversations are extended interactions with multiple turns that focus on building up one or more ideas. By contrast, in most pair-shares and turn-and-talks, each student takes one turn to share an idea with a partner (see

Chapters 4 and 5 for ways to enhance these). In a conversation, one partner might pose an initial idea, and the other partner helps to build it up, asking questions, clarifying, and adding evidence. This co-construction of ideas is vital in effective conversations.

One of the powers of conversation with just one other person is that you always have to be "on" whether you are listening or talking—and you always have to be thinking. You have one other person looking right at you, expecting you to talk or to listen, and expecting you to contribute to the real-time building of your idea(s). You can't space out like you might in a whole-class discussion, a small-group discussion, or even a typical pair-share.

Another power of paired conversation is language development. Every other turn, there is a high concentration of linguistic input that the speaker is trying to make as clear as possible for you. And every other turn you get to (and often have to) put your complex thoughts into oral output for a very real other person listening in real time. You work hard to understand the language of your partner, and you work hard to make your thoughts understood through language.

This section provides enhancements to paired conversation activities that teachers are already using. Yet perhaps the biggest and most challenging enhancements in many classrooms are providing more opportunities to converse in pairs and providing more time in each opportunity. In our zeal to try to "cover" a lot of curricular ground, conversation time often gets squeezed out. Students need to practice every day, every year, and in every discipline in order to build up their expertise in paired conversation. It is a major shift in many settings, but I have never heard any teachers, even after plenty of challenges, tell me they want to go back to giving students less paired conversation time. Here are some enhancements that can help you overcome some of the challenges.

Requires and Helps Students to Purposefully Build Ideas

- Create conversation prompts that inspire and interest students in building up ideas with another person. The ideas should be worth keeping in their heads the rest of their lives. The prompt should motivate and require students to take multiple turns, and it should ask them to clarify and support as much as they can. Think about if you, as an average student, would want to converse about it. A sample prompt is this: "With your partner, clarify and use evidence to build up an idea about how the story and the poem are encouraging readers to be unique and to celebrate differences. You will then write your own story and poem about this or another key theme of your choosing."

- After you have given students the prompt and before they begin their conversations, have students tell each other what they plan to talk about and what they want to get out of the conversation. They can also write this down. They can use or start an idea-building blueprint visual (see Chapter 2 or the online appendix) or some other graphic organizer.

- Show students models of good conversations, analyze the conversational skills in them, and identify what the fictitious students might do to improve the conversation. (e.g., "They should clarify what Alicia meant when she said that it's not worth fighting for it in the long run.").

- Stop the paired conversations halfway through to let students gather their thoughts, take notes, and craft any questions that they might want to ask in the "second half." Have them take stock of whether or not and how well they are responding to the prompt. They can also ask permission from you to alter the prompt if their talk is taking them in a different, yet productive direction.

Requires and Helps Students to Clarify and Support

- Model how to ask for and add to clarity, especially when partners don't share a long response or when they use ambiguous language (e.g., things, it depends, good, bad), by using prompts such as "Do you mean that…?" "Can you explain how…?" "Why…?" Remind students that what they hear is almost never perfectly understood in the way intended by the speaker. We are all different and have different meanings for words and sentences. Clarity is a constant yet necessary struggle.

- Highlight and model, as much as possible, the importance of finding and using the strongest support (evidence, examples, details, reasons) possible to bulk up an idea. Model your thinking as you identify evidence, use criteria to evaluate its strength, and choose which evidence to use in a conversation. Remind students that it is easy to just choose a couple of low-hanging evidence fruits to talk about until time is up. Over time, this builds up bad habits that last throughout life. Imagine using that same slice of time, with more effort and energy, to push for strong evidence and explanations of them. Over the years it will make a huge difference in their thinking, learning, and language.

- Have a third student play the role of an "observer-coach" who observes the paired conversation to (a) keep track of idea building (e.g., take notes on an idea-building blueprint; stack up clarify and support cards with notes on them) and (b) help deepen, direct, or extend the conversation, when needed. At the end, the observer-coach then recaps the idea building for the two conversers, and all three can have a short conversation about what to add or clarify next.

Requires and Helps Students to Fill Information Gaps

- Have the two partners read or watch two different texts before their conversations so that they can share different information with one another as they co-construct ideas. They should have the prompt beforehand so that while reading they can take notes that they will use in the eventual conversation.

- Before the paired conversation, have students respond to the prompt in a pair-share. Then have them write down some notes. Then have them converse, in pairs, with a different partner. This will allow them to get some ideas in the opening pair-share that they can use in their conversations.

- Have students engage in two (or more) successive conversations. After the first one, have them take notes on the current state of their idea or claim, and think about what they will say and ask when conversing with the next partner. Remind them that they should try to make their ideas clearer and stronger in the next conversation, if possible. This is a conversation variation of the Stronger and Clearer Each Time activities in Chapter 5.

- In math, have students work in pairs to create their own problems to help them develop and show the big math ideas. Then have them trade problems with another pair, solve the new one, and build up an explanation of how both problems support their evolving big ideas.

CLASSROOM EXAMPLE: Enhancing Paired Conversations in Fifth-Grade Science

The two versions ask students to pair up and converse about the interactions of Earth systems, such as the geosphere, hydrosphere (including ice), atmosphere, and biosphere. Notice that the original version keeps the focus on the product, while the enhanced version also emphasizes the quality of the conversation.

Original version. After students watched a video and read an article on the topic, the teacher planned to have them pair up and respond to the prompt,

"How do Earth's main systems interact?" She would tell students to have a conversation that would help them create a poster showing their ideas, and then several pairs would share it with the whole class because there would be only enough time for a few whole-class presentations.

Enhanced version. The teacher started by telling students, "Imagine that Earth and the moon can talk. The moon asks, 'So, you seem to have a lot more going on than I do, with all of your fancy systems. Can you describe and show me how they work to keep you healthy? And if there is a problem with them or their interactions, what happens? Where are you most vulnerable?" Then the teacher had students read three different texts on Earth systems and their interactions, with the prompt in mind. In triads, A, B, and C partners each read a text. Partner C became the observer-coach for the first of two conversations. Student C took brief notes on clarify and support cards and stacked them up as A and B talked. At times, C helped to keep the conversation going, but didn't share from her article yet. They all took notes, and then the teacher then announced that Students B and C would talk next and A would be the observer-coach. Here is a sample conversation from the lesson.

A: So what do we need to do?

B: Come up with an answer to the moon about systems, Earth systems.

A: Okay, so the geosphere connects to hydrosphere. Water changes the land.

(C puts a supporting card on the stack.)

B: The hydrosphere is water…

A: And ice.

B: So water and ice change the land. How?

(C puts a clarify card on the stack.)

A: Glaciers, they, a long time ago, cut valleys, big ones.

(C puts a support card on the stack.)

B: But rivers do that too.

(C puts a clarify card on the stack.)

A: Yeah. Is that it?

C: What about atmosphere?

(Continued)

(Continued)

B: Oh yeah.

A: So the water goes up and makes clouds and takes the rain over the land.

(C puts a support card on the stack.)

B: And makes the rivers, and they cut through the land and take dirt into the ocean.

A: I think that makes it salty, right?

B: I don't know. I like swimming in lakes more.

C: Don't forget the biosphere.

A: So, how does it, bio, life connect with the others?

B: I think my article on global warming said something like people put gases into the air and they heat up.

A: No, they go up and trap heat from the sun in the air down here, like a greenhouse.

(C puts a support card and clarify card on the stack.)

B: Oh yeah. Then things heat up and the ice melts—that changes the hydrosphere. Let's draw it.

A: Okay. Yeah. And then the ice melts and floods the land. That's geosphere. That's all of them.

(C puts a card down with the words most vulnerable.)

B: What do you mean?

C: The prompt asked where the earth is most vulnerable if things change too much.

A: I think the greenhouse thing we talked about…

Notice the learning value, the content understandings, and the academic language used in this conversation. The turns weren't very long, but the students did a nice job building up the complex idea that they were trying to build. Student C also helped by stepping in at crucial times when the conversation stalled—but without becoming a full-on third participant.

 ## Enhanced Socratic Seminars

Socratic seminars tend to be discussions that focus on a particularly challenging topic or text. They start by answering an engaging, open-ended question that invites students to share their perspectives with the group. When listening, students should use critical thinking skills and build up their own thoughts to add to the discussion. They should also continue to ask thoughtful and helpful questions that deepen the discussion and focus on answering the question with a robust idea. The teacher prepares for the seminar by choosing an interesting text or set of texts that generate one or more juicy questions, such as "Which historical account is more true?" or "Is war ever justified?" "Is some form of utopia possible?" "Should we spend money to explore space?" "What is quality?" Of course, even better is when students come up with questions to guide the seminar. The teacher reminds students to use their norms for discussion, such as respectfully disagreeing and ensuring that everyone gets a chance to share.

Requires and Helps Students to Purposefully Build Ideas

- At the beginning of the unit, give students a choice of a culminating "show your learning" product that the seminar will help them with (e.g., poster, letter, blog, speech, article, book, website). This gives some extra purpose for talking, listening, and taking notes in the seminar. If needed, pose one or more initial questions that get students hooked into the conversation, and stop at times to brainstorm how the seminar will help them with their projects.

- Remind students that (a) the seminar is not a debate to win but rather a powerful chance to collectively develop important ideas that will stay with them and continue to grow throughout life, and (b) other students have a wealth of knowledge and opinions to share. Before the seminar, have them write down some ideas (e.g., with sticky notes at the top of a blueprint) that they think they want to build by participating in the seminar. You can also give students the topic and potential seminar question(s) beforehand to help them take notes as they read the texts.

- Have one or two people take notes on a visual organizer (e.g., idea-building blueprint, semantic map) or cards to show how the group is building up an idea during the seminar. If there are opposing ideas (i.e., argumentation), have notetakers put two blueprints on opposite sides of a cross beam and weigh them against each other at the end of the conversation (see argument balance scale in Chapter 6).

- Use inner and outer circles. The outer-circle students, often called copilots, sit behind their pilots in the inner circle and listen to their conversation. You can have the class split in two or have even smaller inner-outer groups (e.g., four inner and four copilots). Copilots take notes and can pass notes at times to their pilots in the inner circle. Stop the discussion at times to have pilots pair up with their copilot to synthesize the ideas that have been built up thus far. ("So far, we have established that...") It's like a quick "state of the conversation" to reflect on what else needs to be discussed. This can also happen before the inner and outer circles switch places.

- During the year, encourage students to depend on you less and less to facilitate and lead the discussions. By the end of the year, they should take over most of the guiding and structuring of the process.

Requires and Helps Students to Clarify and Support

- Every time a student (or you) shares a thought that could use some elaboration or support, pause the discussion for all to think about a possible question to ask. Have students think about ways to add a clarifying or supporting "building block" for the idea that connects well to what was just said (e.g., "Great point! And another thing that supports that idea is on page 4 where she said...").

- Ask those in the outer circle to write down possible questions and suggestions to quietly pass to those in the inner circle for use in beefing up the seminar discussion.

- When using inner-outer circles, have students stop, turn, and reflect several times in paired chats, with an emphasis on evaluating how clear and supported the current ideas are. (A copilot might say, "So the idea you all were just discussing needs more support. You could bring up how Columbus met a man on the island who spoke to him in Portuguese.")

Requires and Helps Students to Fill Information Gaps

- Provide three or more texts to all students. Have all students read one main text, and have smaller groups of students read or look at different texts from which they get information that they can share in the seminar. This allows students to be experts on topics in texts that others haven't read.

- Provide different resources to inner and outer circles. Give the outer-circle students helpful information (texts, notes, visuals, etc.) that they need to share orally with inner-circle participants just before the seminar and during "pilot-copilot breaks."

- Pause the group conversation occasionally to have the inner-circle participants get into pairs and come up with the answer to a juicy question just posed (by students or by you), or they can come up with a key question. And the outer-circle copilots can also turn to one another and do the same. If there is time, have pilots meet and share with their copilots before starting up the inner-circle conversation again.

The students in both versions had read Orwell's (1949) *1984* and Bradbury's (1953) *Fahrenheit 451* and had been going back through both books to add to their notes focused on answering the guiding questions that would start off the Socratic seminar: "What are key motifs in the novels?" and "What is the most important theme, shared by both books, that might be relevant for us today?"

Original version. Students had already put sticky notes on the pages that they thought would provide some interesting answers to the guiding questions in the seminar. The teacher planned to have the whole class put their desks in a circle before posing the first question about motifs. The teacher planned to lead the discussion to get them to come up with several thematic motifs, such as conformity vs. individuality and knowledge vs. ignorance. They would ideally discuss how to turn these into clear statements on an important theme that both books shared. Finally, they would use the seminar ideas to write an essay on that theme.

Enhanced version. The teacher started off by asking the class, "Imagine for a moment that our future ends up like the futures in these novels. It's not that hard, really. What should you do and why? Which characters should you become like or not, and why? What life principles would you stick to? Now, let's start by brainstorming some of these principles or themes, which are ideas that we can build up or argue in the seminar. Let's begin by looking at some of the thematic motifs that we have already brought up, such as conformity vs. individuality and knowledge vs. ignorance." Students suggested some additional ideas such as distraction vs. focus and more vs. less governmental control. After giving students time to go back into the novels and take notes, the teacher said, "So before choosing an idea to build up, let's review how we build up ideas." A student says, "By asking questions." The teacher responds, "Yes, for example, you can ask each other questions that do…what? Yes, clarify and support, especially with support from the texts. I want to hear some quotations from the texts, *and* also I want to hear explanations of how they support the idea that you are trying to support."

She continued, "I also want copilots to use the blueprint visual to take notes on the key pieces of evidence and clarifications that we use to build up the ideas. To help you gather your thoughts again, we will have two timeouts during the seminar for copilots to confer with pilots. You can also pass notes to your pilot—*helpful* notes—if you know what I mean. After the first seminar, copilots and pilots switch places to have a second seminar. If you think there is still enough building needed for the first idea, you can continue with it, or you can start up a new idea. I might weigh in at times, if that's okay. Finally, after our seminars I will have you engage in a final conversation with a different partner about the idea or ideas that you built up. You will discuss what you'll put into an op-ed letter to a newspaper about what people need to do and be in order to prevent, counteract, or cope with the types of futures described in the novels. And you also have plenty of real-world examples that you can include in your letters."

Here is a sample excerpt from the Socratic seminar in this enhanced lesson. Look for ways in which the enhancements might have strengthened the discussion. The letter *T* is the teacher and letters *A* through *J* are students.

A: I think we do something for knowledge and ignorance.

B: What about it?

A: We need to be smart.

C: But how does that got to do with the books?

D: I think it's like the government, it doesn't want them, us to be smart.

A: Why not?

D: Maybe because we won't vote for them.

E: My parents say government just takes our money and wastes it.

F: Yeah. (silence)

T: So, copilots, any suggestions? Ten seconds to share with your pilot.
(10 seconds pass)

G: So if we know more about all the bad stuff that the government does, we might vote them out/

E: /Or maybe fight back, like revolution, like the patriots did against England.

T: Let's keep going. It would be nice to hear from someone who hasn't shared, especially if you have a quotation from the text to share that relates to this.

H: I got one from *451*. Beatty tells Montag this: "If the government is inefficient, top-heavy, and tax-mad, better it be all those than that people worry over it. Peace, Montag. Give the people contests they win by remembering the words to more popular songs or the names of state capitals or how much corn Iowa grew last year. Cram them full of non-combustible data, chock them so damned full of 'facts' they feel stuffed, but absolutely 'brilliant' with information." (silence)

B: So, what does that mean?

H: Like the government just wants to fill our heads with useless stuff?

F: I think school is like that.

C: What do you mean?

F: Well, we got these long lists of things we gotta learn. Some of it gets us to think, like this stuff, but a lot is just, I think, filling up our heads so we don't think too much, like all the dates and stuff in history class. (silence)

T: What might be another thing to ask now?

G: What's another example?

I: TV.

A: Can you say more about TV?

I: Yeah. Like the picture walls in the book, in *451*, they use up time, they fill up your brain with, I don't know, nothing. Like his wife, like she was on drugs.

J: Like Facebook or Snapchat. A lot of it is garbage.

T: Okay, nice job. Time for a break-chat with your copilots to talk about what to do next. Maybe you need more support from the text or clarification? For example, in the quotation you discussed was the term *noncombustible data*. What might that mean? Can knowing what it means help?

Notice how several students did teacher-like things to keep the conversation going. There were several well-placed clarifications and supports to help build up the initial idea. And notice how the teacher, even though he was tempted to step in more often, participated only a few times, when needed, mostly to model or guide student facilitation of the seminar. Finally, notice the more engaging prompt and final product in the enhanced version, both of which helped to deepen and give focus to the seminar.

SUMMARY

Conversation is both a goal and a means. We have a responsibility to help students become persons who are great at conversing with a wide range of others about a wide range of topics. And a bonus is that conversation is one of the most powerful ways to develop language, content, critical thinking, and agency. Even though conversations have lots of potential for authentic communication, students often lack a working knowledge of what an effective conversation is supposed to do, and they lack practice in the skills needed for it. Most students need more practice in cosolving problems, cobuilding ideas, and collaboratively arguing with others than they are currently getting in school. For this reason, we must craft lessons that help students develop their skills and learn through conversations.

REFLECTION QUESTIONS

1. How does conversation develop language, content, and thinking in your discipline(s)?

2. How can you weave more conversation into your lessons?

3. Think of a common activity that either intentionally develops conversation skills or depends a lot on conversation. How authentic is it? How strong are the three features of authentic communication? How might it be enhanced?

4. What can you learn from observing student conversations?

USING CREATIVITY TO AMPLIFY AUTHENTICITY

Teaching might even be the greatest of the arts....

—John Steinbeck

To address the challenges of amplifying authentic communication in every lesson, it's not enough to read this book. Even though previous chapters showed how to enhance twenty popular teaching activities, there are many more out there to be enhanced. The enhancement suggestions in this book were not only meant to give you practical ideas for enhancing those specific activities but also to give you examples that you can use as a foundation for creating your own enhancements.

A big challenge in doing this work is that teaching with and for authentic communication does not line up well with many commonly used approaches and even many of the "best practices" in popular curriculum materials and teaching resources. In most settings, a shift to authentic communication requires *major* changes in fostering classroom culture, reading, writing, talking, listening, testing, designing lessons, choosing texts, and assessing. Such changes require large amounts of teacher creativity.

Creativity, in a nutshell, is the process of coming up with a new and useful idea (Sternberg, 1999). *Useful* means that the eventual result, such as an idea, theory, process, method, or product meets some need. *New* means that the creative idea hasn't existed before in a given context. For example, a teacher might come up with the idea of using an analogy of a clogged funnel to clarify a concept in physics. She had never seen or heard of that analogy before; she created it to fit her classroom context. She may bring a funnel into the classroom to further illustrate her point. *Useful* means that the innovation serves a purpose. The teacher had a particular goal in mind when thinking of the funnel analogy. If it works, it was creative. If it doesn't work, it was a creative attempt, or "step," as Thomas Edison called his first 1,100 light bulb trials.

Most creative products and ideas are (a) ways to solve problems shared by a group of people, (b) ways to expand knowledge, or (c) ways to express ideas and thoughts to others. These three purposes exist in abundance every day in every successful school, especially schools where communication powers the learning.

STAGES OF CREATIVITY

Much of the literature on creativity suggests that creativity involves several stages (Brown, 2008; Csikszentmihalyi, 1997; Wallas, 1926). These stages are not necessarily linear, though. Teachers often move back and forth between them while designing lessons, teaching, assessing, and reflecting on what to do next.

Stage I: Immersion and Preparation

This is the stage where we become saturated with experiences, examples, practice, and knowledge of teaching and learning. One of the common myths about creativity is that people either have it or they don't, but research shows that creativity grows out of time spent reading, talking, practicing, and thinking about a particular interest or field. Immersion allows us to become experienced and knowledgeable experts in what *already* exists so that we can then take it in new directions. For teachers, this often means taking close and critical looks at teaching ideas that we use and might use as well as reading avidly about teaching and learning. It means striving to get to know how students think, learn, and communicate. And it means posing big questions about how learning happens most effectively in our setting.

Stage 2: Incubation and Insight

Once we have immersed ourselves in and developed more expertise in teaching, we also learn its problems and complex challenges. Many challenges are either new (students change every year) or so complex that we must let possible solutions *incubate and emerge when they are ready*. This means being open and receptive to whatever insights might come at whatever moment they might come. Often, people describe how their creative ideas have emerged from some kind of repetitive, semiautomatic physical activity, such as showering, driving, and running. These occupy a small portion of the brain and allow the problems and ideas that are swirling around the mind to incubate just beneath conscious levels. In this way, innovative connections form. When the connections become ideas and rise to the surface, creative insights happen.

Stage 3: Choosing

Often, we end up with too many insights, or they might be impractical. We need discernment to choose which to actually pursue and try. Choosing is the process of analyzing how feasible and effective the potential idea will be. At this stage, we separate the good from the bad, the semipossible from the truly impossible. This is the "skeptical stage," in which we ask evaluative questions, such as "Is it worth the time? Has it been tried before? If so, why didn't it work?" Effective choosing is highly influenced by immersion and expertise, in Stage 1. The more expertise we have, the more quickly we can weed out the impractical ideas.

Even after putting ideas through this filter, we rarely have a clear choice. Usually we try out two or three, learn from them, and refine them over time. We may enhance a lesson activity or assessment in a certain way and see how it works. We engage in mini cycles of reflective inquiry in which we use creativity to make changes and try out new ways to see the learning in students.

Stage 4: Disciplined Work

When the creative idea gets chosen in Stage 3, we reach Stage 4, the stage of hard work, perseverance, and intense commitment. This work means putting the idea into practice, trying out variations of it, seeing how well-received it is, and determining if there needs to be any adjustments or further enhancements. For teachers, it also will mean analyzing the idea's results and communicating its value to students, other teachers, administrators, and parents. It takes plenty of time and patience. This is multiyear work and requires bouncing ideas off other colleagues over time to keep improving what we do.

FOUR DIMENSIONS OF CREATIVITY
FOR ENHANCING AUTHENTIC COMMUNICATION

As I worked with teachers on helping them find creative ways to enhance authentic communication in their classrooms, I noticed that there were, roughly speaking, four types of creativity, which I call dimensions, that teachers tend to use: (1) discovering, (2) problem solving, (3) expressing, and (4) interpreting. These dimensions emerged as I worked with creative teachers whose students were engaged, inspired, and successful.

These four dimensions align well with the types of creativity used by engineers, doctors, farmers, lawyers, detectives, screenplay writers, scientists, advertisers, artists, social workers, stage directors, artists, marketers, and other professionals whose work involves solving complex problems. In fact, teachers have many jobs each day: "Today I was an engineer when I prepared the science lab. I was a social worker when I called my students' parents. I was an artist when I made a model story board for tomorrow. I was a detective when I read my students' essays. I was a lawyer when I listened to arguments from two different sides of a student dispute. I could go on, but I have some planning to do for tomorrow, like a city planner." You will see additional comparisons in the four dimension charts in this chapter.

The next four sections describe the four dimensions that teachers can use to increase the quantity and quality of authentic communication in the curriculum. With each brief description of each dimension of creativity, I include a table with several professions that tend to use it, how they use it, and focal questions for teachers. I then provide an example of how a teacher used the dimension to enhance their instruction and assessment for authentic communication. And even though the dimensions are described separately here, it is important to keep in mind that there is a high degree of overlap among them.

I. Discovering

Teachers use creativity to discover things and to expand their knowledge of their field, look at clues, and make inferences about what is going on. We experiment and create new tools for further discovery. We are constantly on the lookout for new methods and connections that might help students learn.

For teachers, discovery has two meanings. The first is discovering who our students are: what they know, how they think, what they want to learn, and how they communicate. Students have a wide range of interests and learning styles that shape their growth and communication methods. We must be creative in getting to know these things about our students each year. Their essays and bubble-in tests tell us just a fraction of who they are and what they are learning and thinking. I have known teachers who hold mini interviews, eat lunch with students, give surveys, exchange letters, play table games, listen to and talk about the music they listen to, and so on.

The second meaning of discovery is uncovering new ways to teach. Education is still in its early stages of development, and we still have much to learn about learning. We must engage in cycles of inquiry over time in order to uncover and then "sculpt" innovative and solid practices that meet our students' communication, content, cognition, and socioemotional needs. And as new ideas, products, and jobs emerge, the field of education must continue to adapt and discover new ideas for thinking about how to best prepare students for the future. See Table 8.1 for specific ways to use this dimension.

Other Profession	How the Profession Creatively Discovers	Teacher Parallels That Foster Authentic Communication
Biologist	Looks for life in strange places; looks for strange life in normal places; observes behaviors under different conditions; understands how life works; looks at and appreciates differences within and across species	How can I discover what motivates my students to put extra energy into talking, listening, reading, writing, conversing, thinking, and learning? How can I improve conditions for authentic communication? How can I appreciate and leverage student differences even when large assessments don't?
Historian	Explores different perspectives of historical figures to understand what happened; looks for bias in sources; analyzes causes and effects of events	How can I step into my students' shoes to create a more engaging lesson on this topic for them? Am I biased in what and how I teach? What are the histories that students enter with?
Cook	Tries new combinations of ingredients and spices	How can I mix together student interests, relationships, standards, assessments, and curriculum materials to create the most engagement and communication possible in every lesson?

Table 8.1   How Teachers Can Use the Creativity Dimension of Discovering to Enhance Instruction

For example, in the beginning of the year a third-grade teacher decided to have students read several short biographies and autobiographies and then write their own personal stories. She included many speaking activities during the unit so she could listen in and discover students' interests and ways of using language. She had students share the highlights of their stories in small groups and then asked students what they learned about their group members. She also discovered, when she experimented with different structures for talking and writing, that having students talk to several different partners in pairs led to clearer and stronger writing.

2. Problem Solving

Solving problems and overcoming challenges may be the most obvious use of creativity as it applies to teaching. Each day we see many problems and challenges of all shapes and sizes already waiting for us when we open the door, just before they begin to pop up spontaneously each hour of the day. For example, a few common problems in many classrooms are (a) having a lack of motivation among students, (b) having a lack of communication between students, and (c) needing to modify purchased curriculum materials to meet the needs of current students. At the core of these problems is the need to know what to prioritize, where to focus our efforts, and how to motivate and instruct students to work productively together.

Also important is training students to creatively solve their own problems. We must avoid "educational enabling," where we quickly hand the answer to the student to save time or rush activities to quickly cover material as dictated in the pacing guide. We must instead creatively scaffold students' abilities and have the patience to wait for students to productively struggle on their own or in collaboration with others. See Table 8.2 for more suggestions.

A sixth-grade teacher, for example, was very concerned that his students didn't seem to care much about using reasoning when they solved problems or when they discussed how math works. Specifically, he was teaching ratios, what they meant, and their practical applications. Students answered minimally and seemed mostly focused on getting right answers. He tackled this problem by thinking about how to get students to "think above" the problems they were solving and the points they were trying to get. This meant that students would use problems to help them build up mathematical ideas. The teacher decided to reframe the problems he would present to students, turning the typical problem-solving task on its head. Instead of giving students problems

Other Profession	How the Profession Creatively Solves Problems	Teacher Parallels That Foster Authentic Communication
Engineer	Tries different calculations to figure out which materials are needed and how to fit all project tasks together within a tight time frame	How do I fit all I that I need to fit into this lesson to help students build ideas and bridge information gaps? How do I effectively organize students for the earth science labs so that they effectively communicate their results and conclusions with others?
Doctor	Uses a variety of diagnostic procedures and treatments to cure a challenging illness; seeks to create a caring system that is as effective as possible	How can I assess a student's current abilities to communicate? How can I get students to go beyond feeling they are required to clarify and support ideas for points?
Social worker	Works with clients to become increasingly confident and self-sufficient; helps them get along with others	How can I best monitor and support students to feel a sense of agency and become independent learners? How can I best foster their social skills as they learn?

Table 8.2 How Teachers Can Use the Creativity of Problem Solving to Enhance Instruction

they needed to "answer," he gave them problems with the answers and asked them to come up with as-clear-as-possible explanations for their small group on (a) how to solve the problem and why to use each procedure and (b) the math concept(s) that the problem was trying to teach them. In every lesson, he emphasizes the importance of building up key math concepts, most of which students put into writing in their journals and performance tasks.

3. Expressing

Effective teachers express ideas and emotions in clear and creative ways. A teacher must use many visual, verbal, and nonverbal symbols of language(s) to communicate a message to a variety of different students, often in large numbers packed into a tight room. And while this communication is often focused on teaching a skill or knowledge, it is also modeling communication skills and strategies.

We must remember that teaching, among other things, is an art form. Art uses a variety of symbols and media to powerfully communicate a concentrated message to others. Painters use figures and colors on a canvas, poets use words and figurative expressions, songwriters use music and words together. Most art has a strong emotional component. It touches and ignites feelings in the receiver, just as teaching does and should.

Clear expression often requires more than just talking. We know this, and yet we still do a lot of just talking because it seems so time efficient. We must be on a constant mission to expand our ways of expressing, including the use of hand gestures, drama, video, images, and music. There are three areas of expression that teachers should continue to develop: (1) expressing the message of the lesson, the essential ideas, and supporting topics; (2) expressing care for, love of, and valuing of students; and (3) expressing one's own personality, interests, and passions. See Table 8.3 for more specific suggestions.

For example, an eighth-grade science teacher wanted to express the idea that the change in an object's motion depends on the sum of the forces on the object and the mass of the object (Next Generation Science Standards [NGSS]

Other Profession	How the Profession Creatively Expresses	Teacher Parallels That Foster Authentic Communication
Author	Makes stories realistic and relevant to life; builds suspense; prompts readers to interpret and ponder	How can I make lessons more like a story in which students want to know what will happen? How can I craft lessons that prompt students to make their own connections and interpretations?
Painter	Uses colors, shapes, composition to convey a message; exaggerates certain features	How do I make a visual of what I want to communicate to my students? What do I emphasize in a lesson, and how? How can I best use color, shapes, and composition of classroom walls and desks?
Architect	Chooses materials that are visually engaging and useful; designs buildings that serve the different needs of many different people	How do I choose the most important materials for helping my students build their skills and ideas? How do I express complex and abstract ideas in a concise way? How do I create learning experiences that build on one another to help students build up key ideas in a discipline?

Table 8.3   How Teachers Can Use the Creativity of Expressing to Enhance Instruction

MS-PS2-2). Instead of putting this standard up on the wall, the teacher put up this question: "What is motion, and what does it depend on?" She told students that they will be going into space soon and will need to know all about motion before they put their astronaut suits on. She then performed several demonstrations and showed several videos of objects in motion and changing their motion. She put a ball on the table and had everyone just watch it sit there; she bounced a tennis ball on a tennis racket, opened a door, and blew up a balloon and let it go. Each time she had students share their evolving answers, and she introduced terms *force, balanced,* and *unbalanced* to help them. To build up and prepare their ideas for presenting to others, she reminded students to refer to examples that they just saw and think up new examples that they could think of or perform in order to communicate their understandings to others.

4. Interpreting

When we interpret something, we use its clues to create a message that is relevant to us. Reading a novel, we might find surprising connections between ourselves and characters who are not like us, giving us new insights into ourselves and our relationship to our world. In teaching, we need to interpret two main categories of clues. The first is interpreting standards and curriculum—figuring out what to teach, how to teach it, and how to assess its learning. Most lists of standards and the curriculums designed to teach them are daunting, consisting of many standards and objectives (not all of which are clearly written), teacher resources, curriculum guides, lesson plans, and assessments. Putting all of these together into a clear and coherent set of lessons is an interpretive challenge that requires creativity.

An important use of this interpretation skill is coming up with big ideas from long lists of standards. In some conversations with teachers, I have even posed what I call the big idea challenge, which asks them to come up with eight to ten big ideas for the year that all the other important things (e.g., standards, facts, skills) connect to and help to build up. So for a high school biology class, for example, a big idea might be this: "Matter and energy are conserved when they flow through and between living systems and the physical environment." Students then build up this idea with the standards that support it. We can still give tests and quizzes to check students' learning of the building blocks, but these assessments should be secondary in importance. The bulk of the focus on learning should be to build up meaty ideas that are vital in the discipline.

The second category is interpreting students' actions and words. With many students and their many communication styles, this challenge is significant. We need to develop this creativity dimension in order to understand what our students need to learn, what they have learned, what they want to learn, how they learn, and who they are. We must be ever careful to avoid quickly jumping to conclusions or placing a student in a box based on a few words, actions, or test scores. We must instead create classroom conditions that allow students to express what they have learned, what they want to learn, how they learn best, and who they are. See Table 8.4 for additional suggestions.

For example, a fifth-grade teacher was pondering the challenge of how to interpret and teach this aspect of the California History-Social Science Framework: "In keeping with the times, they did not ask women to sign [the

Other Profession	How the Profession Creatively Interprets	Teacher Parallels That Foster Authentic Communication
Director of theater or film	Communicates to the audience the feelings of the characters; makes the plot powerful and realistic; involves the audience	How can I use drama to communicate and help students communicate? How can I involve all students in the lesson? How can I set up an interesting challenge, question, or "plot" that will keep students engaged?
Lawyer	Clarifies complex laws and applies them to specific situations; seeks truth and justice; uses evidence to argue; compares each situation to previous cases	What is the essence of what students need to learn? What are the most important "big idea-building" standards? How can I persuade students to see the importance of this learning? How can I apply learning to what they need in future schooling and life? How can I use what I learned about teaching in previous years to teach this year's students?
Archeologist	Digs for answers and deeper questions; makes informed inferences about how and where to look for artifacts; makes connections between them; seeks to be surprised	How can I best gather evidence of my students' needs and learning related to content, thinking, and language? How should I interpret what my student wrote or said? How can I get students to dig into their lives to surprise me with what they know and want to know?

Table 8.4   How Teachers Can Use the Creativity of Interpreting to Enhance Instruction

Mayflower Compact]. This is a powerful opportunity to discuss the meaning of self-government, gender norms in society and religion, and the importance of political rights." The teacher needed to interpret what it meant to discuss the meaning of those ideas, what to highlight, and how to best do this for his twenty-six fifth graders. He decided to use a short mock trial in which a woman argues for her right to sign the Mayflower Compact, starting with an analysis of the expression "In keeping with the times." He made some changes based on the successes and challenges of a mock trial he had done in previous years that focused on John Brown. And he made sure that all students had a chance to participate and show their thinking through oral and written communication before, during, and after the trial. He reminded them that they all had the right to show their learning in ways that they thought were most engaging and provided the best evidence to him, others, and themselves.

CREATING LESSONS

This book has focused more on the activity level within lessons, which I believe is where the enhancements need to happen the most. Yet it is also important to zoom out a bit to think about how we can best fit our enhanced activities together in lessons. There are many decisions, as you know all too well, to be made when designing lessons, such as: Which activities should I include? In which order? How long should they last? How do I connect them and transition between them? How do I formatively assess during them? Which activities do I cut? How can I best provide feedback during them? To answer these and other lesson design questions, we can use one or more of the different dimensions of teacher creativity that are outlined in this chapter.

There are many lesson plan templates and formats out there to choose from. Most tend to follow a "gradual release" model in which students start off the lesson with more support and end it with more independent work. Even some of the longer activities that you saw in previous chapters have this format. Other formats include starting with a question or problem, working toward answering or solving it, and then communicating the answer or solution. You tend to see this more in science and history. In math you can also find lessons starting with a "launch problem" that pushes students to brainstorm and tinker with a challenging problem at the beginning of the lesson. This tinkering provides ideas and discussion topics for the teacher to use to introduce and guide students into the lesson's focus.

In whatever way a lesson is structured, it should have several elements that are grounded in authentic communication. These include the following:

- Activities that have the three features of authentic communication

- Engaging activities that are strategically chosen and organized for this lesson—activities that help students learn what they are supposed to learn (and then some) based on what you have observed in your students

- Activities that build on what students already know and can do

- Activities in which different language modes (reading, writing, listening, speaking, conversing) reinforce one another contentwise and languagewise

- Logical transitions between the activities, including explaining to students why the next activity follows this activity and how it will further help to build up their ideas

- Enough modeling of what students will be asked to do

- Formative observation and adjustment to meet student needs in the moment

There are plenty of other important elements of lessons, but I thought that it would be helpful to highlight these ones here because they focus on authentic communication. When convenient, take some time to think about how effectively your lessons include and embody these elements, and consider how your future lessons might be strengthened.

We shouldn't depend solely on purchased curriculum guides or downloaded lessons because (a) they weren't written with our particular students in mind, and (b) they often lack an emphasis on the features of authentic communication. So it's up to us, using multiple dimensions of creativity, to make the many decisions that help us create the best lessons that we can create in order to serve the needs of all students.

OVERHAULING SYSTEMS

While reading the previous chapters, many of you likely had an important feeling start to emerge that was similar to this one: "I see how this is a major overhaul of how we teach, but it won't be as effective or last very long without larger changes in the overall system."

Yes, we need to also overhaul the system: what and how we assess, what we teach, professional development, how courses are structured, how courses are scheduled, how students are placed in them, etc. We need to cultivate a system that prioritizes authentic communication and engaged learning over collecting points, comparing students, and raising test scores. Many efforts are needed to accomplish this overhaul, but I had room for only five here.

First, leaders at all levels need to be highly creative and strategic in order to transform system features and practices. They need to build relationships, engage in action research, make and alter plans, and take some major risks (e.g., do things that might not cause yearly test scores to go up as much as desired). They need to commit multiple years to this overhaul, which is difficult in many districts that tend to feed on fads from year to year.

Second, we need to realize the limitations that our current systems have for meeting the needs of all learners. Many are multilingual and multicultural students who end up being marginalized and underserved by traditional lessons, curriculums, and assessments. These students tend to bear most of the brunt of carrot-and-stick pedagogies and curriculums that ignore their backgrounds, creativities, and abilities to build up and communicate ideas in a wide variety of powerful ways.

All humans are lifelong language learners. And yet some students who use language that deviates from what school expects tend to be labeled and treated differently than other students. Many are even grouped into separate classes to do tedious language exercises with disjointed content in order to "get their skills up." Instead, we should be valuing their ways of communicating and providing them with numerous opportunities to build up ideas and language with a wide range of peers in school.

Third, we need to trust schools, teachers, and students. The obsession with raising yearly test scores, "closing achievement gaps," and covering standards is, paradoxically, highly detrimental to rich and enduring learning. It hems in and hamstrings what teachers entered the profession to do, which is to work with every fiber of their being to help students reach their potentials. Likewise, we need to trust students to learn things and grow in ways that aren't always visible on the assessments that we give.

We need to realize that the real "achievement gap" is not between the average test scores of different groups of students. It's the gap between the ways in which we are currently teaching and assessing and the ways in which we should be teaching and assessing through authentic communication. It's the gap between a student's current level of academic and personal growth and the growth that he or she could have achieved with more engaging and communication-based instruction. And it's the gap between school systems that support creative, communication-based instruction and school systems that don't. Consider how students can benefit when we learn to close these gaps.

Fourth, we need to learn from others. When possible, collaborate with other teachers, schools, and districts who are engaging in this type of work. Share successes and challenges. I also recommend digging into and discussing resources that focus on project-based learning, culturally responsive instruction, performance-based assessment, social and emotional learning, learning communities, and moving from deficit-based practices to strengths-based practices. Yes, it takes a huge amount of dedication and creativity to weave these together for this major overhaul to happen in your setting, but there's no other way.

Fifth, we must engage in inquiry-based professional development and action research. Many of you already participate in learning communities, team collaborations, and schoolwide initiatives. These are often driven by some inquiry focus that you are trying to answer over time by gathering and analyzing evidence. Perhaps you have come up with several great questions during the course of reading this book. I have included several questions that I still have about communication. Feel free to borrow or adapt any or all of them—and then send me the answers when you have the time.

1. How can we get students to feel uncomfortable when they don't continue to build up a "partially built-up" idea?

2. How can we design and use assessments that focus on building up ideas?

3. How can we shift and adapt curriculum so that it helps students build up important ideas?

4. How can we show that students learn more and better when focused on building up ideas and authentically communicating about them? For example, what indicators for growth in content, language, thinking, socioemotional aspects, and participation should we be looking at?

5. What kinds of enhancements should we make to our reading, writing, listening, speaking, and conversation activities?

CONCLUSION

This and previous chapters covered a lot of ground. Every chapter was focused on helping educators to develop authentic communication features in every activity in every lesson. You saw hundreds of enhancements for twenty activities that are commonly used for classroom learning. You saw dozens of classroom examples across grade levels and content areas in which teachers enhanced activities. And you saw a heavy handful of novel activities in the Going Deeper sections. Hopefully, seeing and trying out some of these suggestions in your setting will help you to build up your creativity and abilities to enhance all that you do with the three features of authentic communication.

For too long we have treated students as consumers of ideas. Instead, our goal should be to see them as architects, engineers, designers, builders, and owners of ideas. It's time to enhance how and what students learn in order to realize this goal. Our students' abilities to learn, create, think, and communicate deserve to be more respected and valued in every classroom. They need to be—and yearn to be—in classrooms where they can build up ideas with others as they also build lasting relationships, language abilities, and social skills.

Please join me and many others out there in working alongside our students, valuing their ideas, celebrating their differences, and nurturing their abilities to communicate with others. It's time to take a stand, which might mean ruffling a few pedagogical feathers. We need to make major changes to immerse students in opportunities to do meaningful things with language and content. When we make these changes, after thirteen years with us, students will end up being very different from the people they would have been after the same amount of time in lessons based on pseudo-communication. Authentic communication has a powerful effect that is well worth the efforts, energy, time, and feather ruffling that are required to shift and overhaul how we teach.

I'll end with a famous quote by Pablo Picasso: "Some transform the sun into a yellow spot; an artist transforms a yellow spot into the sun." We can let narrow-minded policies and hand-me-down practices transform our brilliant children into simple spots (i.e., numbers on a spreadsheet), or we can transform our classrooms and our students into brilliant workshops of ideas, compassion, critical thinking, creativity, and socioemotional awareness.

Adler, C. R. (Ed.). (2001). *Put reading first: The research building blocks for teaching children to read*. Jessup, MD: ED Pubs.

Babbitt, N. (1975). *Tuck everlasting*. New York, NY: Farrar, Straus and Giroux.

Bradbury, R. (1953). *Fahrenheit 451*. New York, NY: Simon & Schuster.

Brown, T. (2008, June). Design thinking. *Harvard Business Review*, pp. 84–92.

Bruner, J. (1996). *The culture of education*. Cambridge, MA: Harvard University Press.

Cazden, C. B. (1977). Concentrated versus contrived encounters: Suggestions for assessment in early childhood. In A. Davies (Ed.), *Language and learning in early childhood*. London, England: Heinemann.

Cazden, C. B. (2001). *Classroom discourse: The language of teaching and learning*. Portsmouth, NH: Heinemann.

Csikszentmihalyi, M. (1997). *Creativity: Flow and the psychology of discovery and invention*. New York, NY: HarperCollins.

Demi. (1996). *The empty pot*. New York, NY: Henry Holt and Company.

Dewey, J. (1916). Thinking in education. *Democracy and education: An introduction to the philosophy of education* (p. 191). New York, NY: The Free Press.

Dewey, J. (1938). *Experience and education*. New York, NY: Macmillan Company.

DiCamillo, K. (2000). *Because of Winn-Dixie*. New York, NY: Candlewick Press.

Duke, N., & Pearson, D. (2002). Effective practices for developing reading comprehension. In A. E. Farstrup & S. J. Samuels (Eds.), *What research has to say about reading instruction* (3rd ed., pp. 205–242). Newark, DE: International Reading Association.

Fox, M. (1993). *Radical reflections: Passionate opinions on teaching, learning, and living*. Boston, MA: Harcourt Brace & Company.

Harmon, J. M., & Hedrick, W. B. (2000). Zooming in and zooming out: Enhancing vocabulary and conceptual learning in social studies. *Reading Teacher, 51*, 155.

Harvey, S., & Goudvis, A. (2007). *Strategies That Work: Teaching Comprehension for Understanding and Engagement*. (2nd ed.). Portsmouth, NH: Stenhouse.

Hughes, L. (1986). Thank you, ma'am. In F. Safier (Ed.), *Impact fifty short stories*. New York, NY: Harcourt Brace Jovanovich.

Husman, J., & Lens, W. (1999). The role of the future in student motivation. *Educational Psychologist, 34*, 113–125.

Keene, E., & Zimmerman, S. (2007). *Mosaic of thought: Teaching comprehension in a reader's workshop*. Portsmouth, NH: Heinemann.

Kelley, M. J., & Clausen-Grace, N. (2010). Guiding students through expository text with text feature walks. *The Reading Teacher, 64*, 191–195.

National Institute of Child Health and Human Development. (2000). *Report of the National Reading Panel. Teaching children to read: An evidence-based assessment of the scientific research literature on reading and its implications for reading instruction* (NIH Publication No. 00-4769). Washington, DC: U.S. Government Printing Office.

Naylor, P. (1991). *Shiloh*. New York, NY: Atheneum Books for Young Readers.

Orwell, G. (1949). *Nineteen eighty-four: A novel*. New York, NY: Harcourt, Brace and Company.

Pintrich, P. (2001). *Motivation in education: Theory, research, and applications*. New York, NY: Prentice Hall.

Sachar, L. (1998). *Holes*. New York, NY: Farrar, Straus and Giroux.

Seligman, M. E. P. (1972). Learned helplessness. *Annual Review of Medicine, 23*, 407–412.

Sternberg, R. (1999). *Handbook of creativity*. Cambridge, England: Cambridge University Press.

Stipek, D. (2002). *Motivation to learn: Integrating theory and practice*. Boston, MA: Allyn & Bacon.

Taylor, M. (1976). *Roll of thunder, hear my cry*. New York, NY: Dial Press.

Thucydides. *History of the Peloponnesian War*.

Vygotsky, L. S. (1978). *Mind in society*. Cambridge, MA: Harvard University Press.

Vygotsky, L. S. (1986). *Thought and language*. Boston, MA: MIT Press.

Wallas, G. (1926). *The art of thought*. London, England: Jonathan Cape.

Wigfield, A., & Eccles, (1992). The development of achievement task values: A theoretical analysis. *Developmental Review, 12*, 265–183.

Wood, D. J., Bruner, J. S., & Ross, G. (1976). The role of tutoring in problem solving. *Journal of Child Psychiatry and Psychology, 17*, 89–100.

Index

Academic listening skills, authentic conversation and, 139

Achievement, true, 12

Achievement gap, real, 177–178

Action research, 178

Actions and words of students, interpreting, 174

Agency
- conversation and, 139, 164
- definition of, 33
- fostering in students, 24, 33–35
- lectures, note-taking, and, 75

Ambiguous language, 155

Anecdotes, 86

Angles and degrees math example
- enhanced version, 104–105
- original version, 104

Archeologists, interpreting dimension of creativity and, 174 (table)

Architects, expressing dimension of creativity and, 172 (table)

Argumentation
- collaborative *vs.* competitive, 142
- in enhanced writing workshops, 113

Argument balance scale, 77, 122, 144
- for argumentation writing, 125–127, 125 (figure)
- enhanced jigsaws and, 95
- 2-D or 3-D version of, 125, 125 (figure)

Arguments, listener requirements for, 75

Articles of Confederation, 101

Authentic communication, 2
- clarifying and supporting ideas, 16, 19–20
- classroom culture and, 23
- deeper learning through, 22
- definition of, 15
- elements in lessons and, 176
- engagement and, 24
- essential purposes of, 3
- filling information gaps, 16, 21–22
- four dimensions for enhancing, 168–175, 169 (table), 171 (table), 172 (table), 174 (table)
- language scaffolding and, 22
- major classroom changes in shift to, 165
- major roles of, in school, 5–6
- messiness and, 40
- moving from pseudo-communication to, 15
- nurturing student voice and, 34

powerful effect of, 179

prioritizing, 177

purposefully building one or more ideas in, 16–19

robust uses of language and, 42

strengthening signs of, 37–38

student's sense of control and, 34

three features forming backbone of, 16–22

See also Conversing, authentic; Listening, authentic; Reading, authentic; Speaking, authentic; Writing, authentic

Authenticity challenge, 1–9

Authors, expressing dimension of creativity and, 172 (table)

Author's press conference, 117

Avoidance strategies, used by students, 87

Back-and-forth conversations, advantages of, 138

Backchanneling, 143

Background knowledge
- in comprehension processes model for listening, 67 (figure)
- in comprehension processes model for reading, 47, 47 (figure)

Because of Winn-Dixie (Dicamillo)
- enhanced version, of teacher read-aloud, 74
- original version, of teacher read-aloud, 73

Bias, 77, 142, 151

"Big idea breaks," 103

Big idea challenge, 173

Bill of Rights, 101

Biologists, discovery dimension of creativity and, 169 (table)

Body language, 86

Body movements, 144

Brainstorming, 124, 126, 145, 175

Brown, John, 175

Bruner, Jerome, role of social interaction and, 3–4

California History-Social Science Framework, interpreting and teaching, 174–175

Cause-effect, in informational texts, 71

Cazden, Courtney, student-initiated discourse and, 4

Chimes, 90

Choosing stage, in creativity, 167

Cisneros, Sandra, 51

A SAGE Publishing Company

Helping educators make the greatest impact

CORWIN HAS ONE MISSION: to enhance education through intentional professional learning.

We build long-term relationships with our authors, educators, clients, and associations who partner with us to develop and continuously improve the best evidence-based practices that establish and support lifelong learning.

Solutions YOU WANT | Experts YOU TRUST | Results YOU NEED

EVENTS >>> **INSTITUTES**

Corwin Institutes provide large regional events where educators collaborate with peers and learn from industry experts. Prepare to be recharged and motivated!

corwin.com/institutes

ON-SITE PD >>> **ON-SITE PROFESSIONAL LEARNING**

Corwin on-site PD is delivered through high-energy keynotes, practical workshops, and custom coaching services designed to support knowledge development and implementation.

corwin.com/pd

>>> **PROFESSIONAL DEVELOPMENT RESOURCE CENTER**

The PD Resource Center provides school and district PD facilitators with the tools and resources needed to deliver effective PD.

corwin.com/pdrc

ONLINE >>> **ADVANCE**

Designed for K–12 teachers, Advance offers a range of online learning options that can qualify for graduate-level credit and apply toward license renewal.

corwin.com/advance

Contact a PD Advisor at (800) 831-6640 or visit www.corwin.com for more information

Made in the USA
Monee, IL
30 May 2023

34953134R00116